INCLUSIVE COLLEGIALITY AND
NONTENURE-TRACK FACULTY

# new FACULTY MAJORITY

# INCLUSIVE COLLEGIALITY AND NONTENURE-TRACK FACULTY

## Engaging *All Faculty* as Colleagues to Promote Healthy Departments and Institutions

## Don Haviland, Jenny Jacobs, Nathan F. Alleman, and Cara Cliburn Allen

Foreword by Adrianna Kezar
Series Foreword by Maria Maisto

The New Faculty Majority series

STERLING, VIRGINIA

Published by Stylus Publishing, LLC.
22883 Quicksilver Drive
Sterling, Virginia 20166-2019

**Library of Congress Cataloging-in-Publication Data**
The CIP data for this title have been applied for.

13-digit ISBN: 978-1-62036-644-8 (cloth)
13-digit ISBN: 978-1-62036-645-5 (paperback)
13-digit ISBN: 978-1-62036-646-2 (library networkable e-edition)
13-digit ISBN: 978-1-62036-647-9 (consumer e-edition)

Printed in the United States of America

All first editions printed on acid-free paper
that meets the American National Standards Institute
Z39-48 Standard.

Bulk Purchases

Quantity discounts are available for use in workshops and for staff development.
Call 1-800-232-0223

First Edition, 2020

*To Kelly Ward*

# CONTENTS

# FOREWORD

*Inclusive Collegiality and Nontenure-Track Faculty: Engaging* All Faculty *as Colleagues to Promote Healthy Departments and Institutions* could not come at a better time. Campuses are recognizing the need to support the growing numbers of nontenure-track faculty (NNTF) and to include them in the life of the campus. The notion of collegiality as it relates to NTTF has been rarely considered and certainly not explored in any detail as is done in this valuable text. Collegiality is central to a healthy work environment and particularly significant for professionals whose work is interdependent. This book offers valuable insights into understanding the many ways *collegiality* is important and provides a helpful definition of this sometimes elusive, often spoken about, and commonly misunderstood concept. The authors push us to move today's current focus on policy to softer issues that deeply shape NTTF's experience and ability to work and perform optimally. The focus for this book came from being challenged by institutional leaders at a presentation in which they showcased data about NTTF not being treated in a collegial manner and asked what to do about this problem. And we do need answers about how institutions can be better—which is what is presented in this book.

The authors provide important insights by examining healthy departments that exhibit collegiality, serving as a source of inspiration and offering transferable lessons for other departments and institutions. By identifying departments at two very different institutions—a public, unionized master's institution and a private, nonunionized research university—the authors explore the complex ways the different contexts shape collegiality through disciplinary norms, departmental histories, physical spaces, and other key aspects that are often overlooked. In my own work aimed at helping campus leaders develop better policies and practices to support NTTF, I have also identified that context is extremely important for developing appropriate policy changes. The corollary is that there is not a one-size-fits-all way to reshape departments to be more collegial. I am struck, however, that collegiality is far more generalizable in terms of principles—which the authors offer at the end of this book—that can be implemented to create greater civility and respect among colleagues rather than policies in support of NTTF.

I so appreciate that the recommendations were specifically addressed to different groups—administrators, department chairs, tenure-track faculty, and NTTF themselves. Being broken up by various groups makes recommendations much more actionable. In addition, the principles the authors offer at the end are an excellent distillation of their research, a way to capture key recommendations about an issue that can be difficult to pin down. Presume inclusion, be sure to reach out and invite NTTF, expand notions of expertise, and nurture and model collegiality: These are all the type of principles that can be embraced by faculty and administrators at various levels to improve the environments of specific departments and campus more broadly. The chapters leading up to these principles offer detailed suggestions about the ways to develop trust and respect and recognize professional expertise. Simple things like keeping one's door open so NTTF can come in to ask questions about classes or students, making awards available to NTTF, including NTTF on committees related to their areas of expertise, and appreciating their support of a committee where they serving are all ways to signal recognition and move toward collegiality. This book is full of small but powerful ways to make NTTF feel respected and included and to improve the work life in departments.

The authors also challenge us to rethink our traditional notions of collegium and expand our understandings of scholarship and of expertise. Throughout this book, readers are asked to rethink our views and conceptualizations of everyday practices that slight NTTF. While the focus of this book is on full-time NTTF, it made me think about how important it is to also have this same exploration into part-time faculty whose relationship is even more tenuous but collegiality is equally important in many ways for this group. I hope to see work on part-time faculty in the future.

Readers will leave this book challenged in terms of their day-to-day views of collegiality, enriched with new approaches for working with colleagues, and armed with concrete steps and recommendations leaders across campus can take to improve collegiality. They will also appreciate the complexity and nuance involved in addressing unhealthy environments and moving to healthier ones; understand the key role of certain individuals such as department chairs to change; and, most importantly, they will have a much better sense of the life of NTTF.

Adrianna Kezar
Dean's Professor of Higher Education
Director of the Delphi Project on the
Changing Faculty and Student Success
University of Southern California

New Faculty Majority (NFM): The National Coalition for Adjunct and Contingent Equity was established in 2009 for one purpose: to focus on resolving the economic, ethical, political, and educational crises created by the shift to a predominantly contingent faculty workforce in higher education. The shift has occurred over decades, and it has led to an institutionalization of attitudes and policies toward contingent faculty members and toward faculty work more generally that must be described as counterproductive at best, exploitative at worst. By denying basic professional working conditions and opportunities for professional growth to faculty members without whom, ironically, higher education could not function, college and university leaders harm students and undermine the common good. Faculty working conditions are student learning conditions, so when faculty are not supported—not provided basic supports from offices to access to professional development—students are not supported. Similarly, when contingent faculty do not have academic freedom protections to ensure that they can challenge students and maintain high academic standards, they cannot fully carry out their duty to educate students to be active, responsible, discerning, courageous citizens.

This series gives members of the academic community an opportunity to wrestle with these vexing, critical issues and to explore real-world, practical, and ethical solutions. It will invite different audiences to be challenged and inspired to think; to collaborate; and yes, to argue, in a way that is true to the diversity of experience that shapes us. Most important, this series will highlight the voices and perspectives of contingent faculty themselves, so that all members of the higher education community committed to quality and equity can work toward these goals with integrity and in good faith.

NFM's objective from the beginning was to create a broad coalition of constituencies including faculty, students, parents, staff, administrators, labor activists, higher education organizations, and community members who would engage in inside/outside education and advocacy. Early in its existence, NFM realized that the project it had taken on was daunting in the same way that the crisis of climate change is so frustrating; namely, that there was significant denial among people who should know better that the problem exists; it is man-made, and, therefore, it requires intentional, dedicated, and honest attention and effort to correct. This series is one important part of the effort to ensure that the climate of higher education is always as conducive to justice as it is to success.

Maria Maisto
President
New Faculty Majority

# ACKNOWLEDGMENTS

We have many people to thank for helping us to bring this book to life. First, we are indebted to our participants from both phases of our research, who entrusted their experiences and insights to us so that we might share them with you. It is particularly encouraging for us, as researchers of collegiality, to know that we have many fine colleagues working at the two institutions that were part of this study. The faculty and administrators with whom we spoke were generous with their time and their thoughts. Moreover, almost uniformly they were earnest and honest in seeking to help us learn how we can improve the collegiality experienced by nontenure-track faculty (NTTF). They wanted to make their departments, institutions, and the profession better, healthier spaces, and we value the gift of their time and energy in doing so.

Second, we are especially appreciative of the NTTF who spoke with us over the two phases of the study. As a marginalized and vulnerable faculty subgroup, NTTF, particularly those who shared negative experiences, took some level of risk in participating in this research. Although we have taken care to protect them, we nonetheless acknowledge their willingness to take a risk, step up, and share their experiences so that change and improvement can happen.

Third, a special note of thanks to our families and friends for their support of this project. Your collective patience (as we disappeared for team meetings and writing binges), encouragement, and general love and support are the foundation from which this sort of work can be accomplished. Thank you!

Fourth, a huge thanks to our editor, John von Knorring. Thank you for your patience in waiting for this manuscript; we hope it was worth the wait! And thank you for your careful reading of our drafts, your general guidance, and your skill at nudging and prodding us to push just a little bit harder on the data related to the relationship between collegiality and diverse social identities. The field has more work to be done in this regard, but our small contributions in this area come in part from your willingness to challenge us to say more.

Finally, we dedicate this book to our dear professional colleague Kelly Ward, who left this world far too early. Kelly was the discussant at the 2015 conference where the anonymous provost asked the question that would lead to this book. She was quick to encourage us to publish our findings and just as quick to push us to do more related to diversity in our findings. In the time after that conference, she was part of our journey in this work, as we had the privilege of engaging in an ongoing dialogue with Kelly on this topic. Throughout, she pushed us, challenging us to develop a more inclusive notion of *collegiality* than traditional definitions might suggest. Kelly pressed us to adopt a more critical lens to acknowledge that the concept of collegiality was built for a White male professoriate and must necessarily evolve to honor the increasingly diverse professoriate. Kelly's words and worldview were frequently on our minds during our team meetings, and we hope this book has done justice to all that she shared with us. We are grateful to have crossed paths with Kelly, and our work is better for having known her.

# 1

## INTRODUCTION

*It's clear that the tenure track is . . . the key to the realm. It's what we're expected to do to fully participate in the university. . . . I think as much as we value people not on tenure, as much as really anyone logically knows we can't run the university without people doing the business of teaching, or doing the clinical work in the professions, there is still that 'separate but not quite equal' mentality.—Joy, NTTF, Research University*

*They always smile, they always say 'hello.'. . . [But] I know my place. The peasant can't eat with the king and queen.—Karen, NTTF, Master's University*

This book grows out of a brief moment at a conference presentation. It was November 2015 and we had finished a talk on the experiences of *full-time nontenure-track faculty* (NTTF). In our presentation we shared stories of marginalization, insults, and passive-aggressive behavior experienced by the NTTF we interviewed. We also shared stories of professional and personal kindness, inclusion, and faculty and administrators who found creative ways to include NTTF as colleagues even when organizational policies and structures made doing so difficult. Our comments were well received, and the problems we posed were met by sympathetic nods.

As the session moved into a discussion, an audience member we later learned was a provost raised his hand and gently asked, "That's all good. So, what do I do about this? How do I make it better?" We paused, offered one or two rough ideas, and realized immediately this was the key question. Studying the problem and its importance was one thing, offering solutions and models for what might work was another. Thus began the journey toward this book.

In the pages that follow, we answer the question posed by the anonymous provost and offer guidance in terms of strategies, policies, practices, and new conceptualizations for those seeking to build more collegial climates for NTTF. Doing so is, we believe, essential for the health of the faculty profession and higher education.

The steady growth in the percentage of faculty who are defined as *contingent* (full- or part-time) over the last several decades is well documented. While just 22% of all faculty fell into that category in 1969 (Kezar & Maxey, 2013), that figure had grown to 70% by 2015 (U.S. Government Accountability Office, 2017). While the faculty as a whole grew by 63.5% between 1995 and 2011, full-time contingent faculty (i.e., NTTF) grew 109%, part-time contingent grew 100%, and tenure-track faculty (hereafter: TTF) grew just 10% (U.S. Government Accountability Office, 2017). And while the reliance on contingent faculty is perhaps most pronounced at for-profit institutions, where they compose more than 99% of the faculty, contingent faculty are quite prominent at 4-year institutions (61%) and 2-year institutions (84%; U.S. Government Accountability Office, 2017). More specifically as it relates to this book, estimates put NTTF at between 20% and 25% of the full-time faculty workforce (Kezar & Maxey, 2013), with use of NTTF most pronounced at research universities (more than 24% of faculty) and comprehensive universities (more than 11%) as of 2007 (Ehrenberg & Zhang, 2005; Kezar & Maxey, 2013; Kezar, Maxey, & Eaton, 2014). A 2018 American Association of University Professors (AAUP) report noted that in 2016, institutions nationally hired nearly 50% more NTTF than TTF (30,865 NTTF to 21,511 TTF).

NTTF in particular can have a profound impact on the academic success of students because they teach such large numbers of undergraduates and a substantial number of graduate students as well. In an analysis of the use and status of contingent faculty, the Government Accountability Office (GAO; 2017) found that contingent faculty in 3 states selected for in-depth analysis teach up to 54% of the courses at 4-year public institutions, including anywhere from 25% to 33% of lower division courses, and 25% of upper division in the 3 states sampled. A 2014 AAUP analysis found that NTTF delivered 50% more hours of instruction than TTF at research universities and 15% more hours at other 4-year institutions. One study found that undergraduates at a particular doctoral-extensive university had, on average, 36% of their credits taught by NTTF (Jaeger & Egan, 2011). NTTF are often the first point of contact students have with a possible major (with the potential to pull those students in or push them away from the major) as well as for key general education courses that might affect time-to-degree.

Despite the growing presence and significant role of NTTF, the faculty profession and higher education institutions are only just beginning to grapple with how to better integrate them as the structure of the faculty continues to evolve. The general sense of dissatisfaction and marginalization of NTTF is well documented. NTTF are often unhappy about the nature of their interactions with colleagues (Alleman & Haviland, 2016; Hearn & Deupree, 2013; Hollenshead et al., 2007; Levin & Shaker, 2011; Ott & Cisneros, 2015; Waltman, Bergom, Hollenshead, Miller, & August, 2012), their disconnection from the department curriculum (Umber, 2014), and their exclusion from decision-making spaces (Haviland, Alleman, & Cliburn Allen, 2017; U.S. Government Accountability Office, 2017). The net result of this marginalization is wasted human capital, with NTTF often excluded from key spaces and conversations despite their significant contact with students and impact on academic programs.

As we describe later in this chapter, this state of affairs reflects a breakdown in collegiality, a cornerstone value of faculty culture and a central component of academic governance (Bergquist & Pawlak, 2008; Bess, 1992; Birnbaum, 1988; Gappa, Austin, & Trice, 2007). More than simply being nice, collegiality is about prosocial behaviors (Bess, 1992) that facilitate a larger purpose: professional and humane interactions during times of potential conflict, such as curriculum reform, hiring, and creation of academic policy (Alleman & Haviland, 2014). It is this spirit of collegiality that underpins governance and service, with a focus on consensus and the good of the institution (or department, college, etc.), and a priority on decision-making that is deliberative and inclusive of the interests of colleagues—even if those colleagues are not present in the deliberations (Bess, 1992). A breakdown in collegiality for the faculty body or for a category of faculty such as NTTF is thus problematic, to say the least. Our goal in this book, then, is to offer ways to mend this break.

Our book is based on extensive data collection at 2 institutions over a 5-year period. We began, as noted previously, by examining the problem; we heard both positive and very disturbing stories of NTTF's experiences with collegiality. Then, accepting the challenge from the provost in our conference session, we focused on studying departments that were identified as being "healthy" environments in terms of collegiality for NTTF. Doing so helped us see how some departments are able to navigate and negotiate shaping collegial environments with an increasingly differentiated faculty. All told, we have spoken with 101 individuals (NTTF, TTF, department chairs, and administrators) about collegiality for NTTF. Doing so has helped us not only understand NTTF experiences but also gain a richer understanding of what TTF, chairs, and administrators can do as gatekeepers to foster more collegial spaces for NTTF. In the chapters that follow, we share what we have learned from those people and places where collegiality for NTTF (and faculty more generally) is present.

In the remainder of this chapter, we develop and expand on the ideas presented in the preceding paragraphs. We look more closely at who NTTF are and the roles they play in the university. Next, we provide a brief but more detailed discussion of collegiality and its importance, to provide a foundation for the rest of the book. We then review the very conditional or limited experiences NTTF have with collegiality and explain why this limited access to collegiality is problematic. We close the chapter with an overview of the main ideas in the remainder of the book.

## NTTF and Collegiality in U.S. Higher Education

As we begin to look more deeply at NTTF, it bears repeating that we are focusing on full-time NTTF. We do so because their presence and work, as we will see, most closely resembles that of TTF. Given the full-time nature of the work and the heavy (but not exclusive) focus on instruction, NTTF are likely to be on campus as much as or more than TTF and thus be engaged with students, colleagues, and administrators in ways that more closely resemble TTF than part-time faculty. Moreover, while not uniform, NTTF often have similar professional preparation and socialization and therefore expect their experiences as faculty to be similar to their TTF colleagues (Kezar, 2013a; Ott & Cisneros, 2015). A gap between these expectations and experiences would therefore seem to be particularly problematic both for NTTF and their institutions.

The NTTF role emerged and has grown for a variety of reasons. The increasing professionalization of the faculty role in the twentieth century is closely linked to academic specializations; departments and professional associations; and, ultimately, research (Clark, 1987; Rice, 1986; Wagoner & Kellams, 1992). With growing rewards for TTF to engage in scholarship and increasing pressure to generate external funding came less time for and focus on instruction; the NTTF role emerged to fill that gap. This trend has joined with increasingly constrained fiscal resources, a relatively robust supply of PhD-level labor, and a desire for more programmatic and fiscal flexibility (Baldwin & Chronister, 2001; Cross & Goldenberg, 2009; Golde & Dore, 2001) to further differentiate the faculty role—with NTTF as one solution. The traditionally integrated faculty role (teaching, research, service) declined as faculty work roles began to split in pursuit of efficiency (Finkelstein & Schuster, 2011). By 1993, NTTF constituted the majority of full-time faculty hires (Schuster & Finkelstein, 2006).

However, given the growing complexity of the multiversity, the nature of NTTF work itself has also become more complex and, in many cases, increasingly mirrors work done by TTF. Teaching continues as a significant part of NTTF responsibilities; however, and perhaps not surprisingly, given the similarities in preparation and institutional needs, NTTF work has shifted over time toward that of TTF to include teaching, scholarship, and service (Hollenshead et al., 2007; Kezar, 2013a; Kezar & Sam, 2011). Indeed, NTTF often coordinate undergraduate programs, shape recruitment and admissions practices, handle scheduling, secure grants, and engage in scholarship, thus influencing the student and faculty experience in myriad ways (Alleman & Haviland, 2016; Haviland et al., 2017; U.S. Government Accountability Office, 2017).

NTTF hiring has eclipsed TTF hiring for some time, which means that to the extent that there have been improvements in the diversity of the faculty, much of it has been in the NTTF ranks. For instance, the percentage of women in NTTF roles grew from 35.5% to 44.3% between 1990 and 2006. Similarly, between 1993 and 2013, the growth of minoritized faculty in the NTTF role (143%) far exceeds the growth of these groups in tenured (60%) and tenure-track (30%) lines (Finkelstein, Conley, & Schuster, 2016). The most recent National Center for Education Statistics (2018) data from fall of 2017 show that NTTF ranks saw a 94.8% increase in diverse faculty while TTF ranks saw an increase of 84.4% (U.S. Department of Education, National Center for Education Statistics, 2018, Table 315.20).

To some degree, the presence of NTTF has become normalized, even if the nature of their work and roles is not consistently or clearly defined. A 2018 AAUP analysis found that NTTF enjoyed, not surprisingly, more job security than their part-time peers: 58% of NTTF at 4-year universities were on multiyear or indefinite contracts, and 38% had annual contracts (American Association of University Professors, 2018). The at-will nature of some contracts provides institutions with the staffing flexibility they seek. However, these contracts can often evolve into more permanent contracts where NTTF can only be terminated for cause, making the NTTF nearly as secure as tenured faculty (U.S. Government Accountability Office, 2017). The growing institutionalization of the NTTF position points to the fact that NTTF have a growing and significant role in higher education.

Although there is a growing push to integrate NTTF into departmental and institutional structures rather than seeing them as a threat to the tenure system (Baldwin & Chronister, 2001; Kezar, 2012, 2013c; Kezar & Maxey, 2015; Kezar & Sam, 2010a, 2010b), and despite the similarities in both preparation and work functions, NTTF often have workplace experiences that are substantially different from their TTF peers. Scholars talk about NTTF as experiencing a dualistic career (Levin & Shaker, 2011), generally respected as experts and scholars by their students but getting little respect from or engagement with colleagues (Hearn & Deupree, 2013; Hollenshead et al., 2007; Levin & Shaker, 2011; Ott & Cisneros, 2015; Waltman et al., 2012). Institutions typically do much less to recruit and orient NTTF than TTF and provide limited professional development that, when it is present, focuses more on institutional needs (e.g., effective teaching) than on NTTF professional needs and goals (Kezar & Sam, 2010b).

Our own research has uncovered a host of structural problems, contradictions, and inconsistencies that reflect the marginalization NTTF often experience from their faculty colleagues. Although there is substantial variation, some NTTF described being able to sit on curriculum committees while others said they could not; some said they could contribute to curriculum (even if they could not be on a committee), while others developed curriculum but had to have it submitted under the name of a TTF. Some were official coordinators of programs, and others did the work behind the scenes while a TTF held the title. Some NTTF described being consulted about scheduling department meetings while others were completely left off electronic mailing lists that communicated the date/time of department meetings and other relevant content.

Beyond these kinds of structural issues, our research has revealed multiple examples of microaggressive behavior such as exclusion from social events like lunches, holiday parties, and retirement celebrations. Other examples included the following:

- One participant was an active scholar and had presented a well-received conference paper. His chair complimented him with, "That was an awesome paper. No one would ever guess you went to a shit school."
- A faculty participant described asking for a door sign that had her "Dr." title on the door, to match that of the male NTTF in the office next to her. The department instead changed the male's door sign, removing "Dr." from his nameplate and marginalizing both.
- One NTTF described being in her office with her door open as the department chair gave a tour to some guests. As the group walked by, the chair said, "I'd introduce you to some faculty members, but nobody is here right now."

Ultimately NTTF in our studies, and in the literature more generally, are often marginalized in their departments. Even within healthy departments, their access to positive social interactions, engagement as team members, and decision-making structures can be uneven and idiosyncratic at best. Excluded structurally by policy and practice, as well as culturally by virtue of the exceptions in a tenure-normative system, engagement and inclusion of NTTF, to the extent they occur, are driven often by the goodwill of chairs or other TTF and some institutional administrators. We view this state of affairs as a breakdown in collegiality—a concept to which we turn next.

## What Is Collegiality?

*Collegiality* (and derivatives, e.g., *colleagues*) is a word often used in higher education but also a "squishy" term not well understood. Scholars (e.g., Bess, 1992; Cipriano, 2011; Gappa et al., 2007) have provided varied conceptualizations and definitions of *collegiality*. Based on these definitions as well as our own work, we have boiled the term down to the following key points:

- *Shared mission and purpose*: Collegial environments are grounded in a sense of shared mission and purpose, with a commitment to problem-solving based on a sense of the common good, because individuals are all pulling in the same direction.
- *Sense of team*: In collegial spaces, there is a general sense of team and cohesion, grounded in both interpersonal knowing as well as a sense that relationships are likely to be long term and thus worthy of investment.
- *Good neighbors*: Individuals in collegial environments have a sense of familiarity and trust because they know each other. Thus, they feel confident making decisions based on the shared mission rather than from an expectation of reciprocity or quid pro quo or a desire to protect their individual interests.
- *Open exchange of information*: Members of collegial environments engage in an open exchange of information, consult with one another regularly without regard to hierarchy, and are both willing and free (i.e., not punished) to name organizational problems.
- *Participatory decision-making*: In collegial spaces, deliberations and decisions take place in an atmosphere of support and inclusion, with a desire to make rational decisions based upon consensus.

Foundational to the principles we describe is *respect*, which Gappa, Austin, and Trice (2007) describe as "a fundamental entitlement for every faculty member" (p. 139), with no differentiation between TTF and other faculty.

As we have engaged in our work, we have come to recognize that respect has both personal and professional components that shape the collegial experiences of NTTF (and all faculty). This conceptualization underpins the organization of this book. On the personal side, which we call *interpersonal trust and respect*, in collegial environments faculty are recognized as human beings with aspirations, dignity, accomplishments, goals, and talents. This idea of human regard speaks to the importance of personal relationships in faculty work, for these relationships form the basis of the trusting, prosocial interactions (Bess, 1992; Tierney, 2008) that are a pillar of collegiality. This sense of interpersonal trust and respect comes through most clearly in the daily personal interactions among faculty—the simple hello in the hallway, interest in one's partner or children, curiosity about a new passion project, and shared social events.

On the professional side, collegial environments are a space where faculty recognize the *professional expertise* of those with whom they work. Respect for professional expertise speaks to the regard faculty hold for one another related to their potential to make contributions to the shared mission as well as to participate in and contribute to deliberations and decision-making. Recognition (or lack of it) for professional expertise is typically evident in institutional policies (e.g., on what committees one can serve, who gets to vote and when) and practices (e.g., sharing of information, allocation of office space) that illustrate the degree to which one's professional expertise is honored.

The model in Figure 1.1 reflects our conceptualization of the elements that shape collegial experiences. As the figure shows, the foundation for collegiality comes from a blend of interpersonal trust and respect and the recognition of expertise within the context of a department, college, school, or institution. As the arrows in the figure indicate, there is an iterative nature to this process, with collegiality promoting the kinds of prosocial interactions that, in turn, contribute to interpersonal trust and respect and recognition of expertise.

While some behaviors or practices may distinctly reflect interpersonal trust and respect or recognition of professional expertise, other behaviors or practices may reflect both dimensions. Take, for example, inclusion. Inclusion has a personal dimension, with open doors and hallway conversations and invitations to lunches and social events facilitating interpersonal knowing. At the same time, inclusion related to things like committee service, department meetings, and voting are organizational reflections of regard for professional expertise. Thus, these dimensions are reflected as a Venn diagram to indicate the overlap between the two.

Finally, context is a critical element in shaping collegial experience. Disciplinary norms and cultures can play a significant role in how NTTF are perceived and regarded. For instance, our own work suggests that NTTF are generally more integrated in professional fields, which value the

**Figure 1.1.** Elements contributing to collegial experiences for faculty.

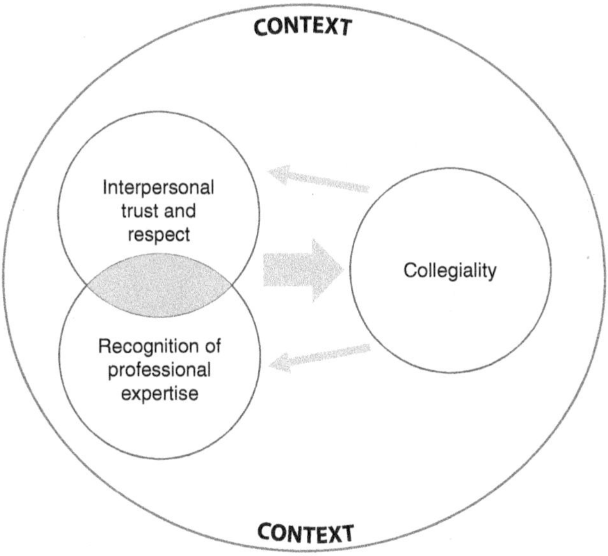

practice-based experience and expertise that NTTF bring to the university. Beyond this example, other contextual factors, such as department size, facilities (e.g., use and location of office space), and history of leadership, can also shape the NTTF experience with collegiality.

As we noted, collegiality has important organizational implications that reach beyond simply having people "get along." Collegiality bestows upon faculty both rights and responsibilities (Mangiardi & Pellegrino, 1992). All colleagues, even the most junior, have the right to be heard and to shape decisions, as well as access to information, for instance (Bess, 1992; Birnbaum, 1988; Clark, 1987; Hardy, 1991). At the same time, collegiality comes with responsibilities, including the duty to participate in institutional governance, treat one another with kindness, trust one's colleagues, and identify organizational concerns (Bess, 1992; Bowen & Schuster, 1968). The ideal results of collegiality, then, include faculty who engage with each other in service to the institution and its mission.

We end this section with one caution: Collegiality can be a problematic concept when misunderstood or misused. We were reminded of this idea when we heard a state educational leader describe collegiality as stifling debate, disagreement, and programmatic change. We saw evidence that some view and even enact collegiality this way even in our study of healthy departments. For example, one faculty member described concerns that an institutional turn toward pursuing initiatives and goals related to diversity and advocacy for minoritized groups was disrupting collegiality among faculty across the campus. (We were also relieved to note that several participants from the same institution expressed concern over a faculty petition that circulated throughout the campus to remove an administrator who was responsible for diversity initiatives on campus, noting the argument that unity was being disrupted by diversity was particularly problematic for the pursuit of collegiality.) However, based on the definition we have offered, this interpretation of *collegiality* as stifling debate and diversity of views is the antithesis of collegiality, where transparency and honesty provide the foundation to identify and solve organizational issues.

Similarly, we are mindful that behavior under the guise of collegiality can be and has been used to exclude rather than include those (e.g., women and other minoritized faculty) who might not reflect a once-homogenous (i.e., White, male) faculty body. Much like the problematic concept of *fit*, a misapplied notion of collegiality can marginalize others as so-called poor colleagues when, in fact, it is those making the accusations who are undermining the collegial ideal. It might be true that collegiality today, with an increasingly diverse faculty, is more complicated than in years past (Haviland et al., 2017). However, this diversity and complexity make the pursuit of the collegial ideal all the more important.

## NTTF and Collegiality: What's Causing the Problem?

The concept of expertise is central to understanding NTTF's highly conditional access to collegiality. As we have noted in our earlier work (Haviland et al., 2017), this access to collegiality takes place in a space known as the collegium. Downey (1996) defines the *collegium* as a "complex network of assumptions, traditions, protocols, relations, and structures" (p. 75) that forms the basis of faculty legitimacy in terms of academic governance. Access to this space, and the rights and responsibilities of collegiality, is granted over time as one's professional expertise is recognized by one's peers. The access is regulated based on standards and criteria of selectivity and elitism (Petro, 1992; Prieber, 1991) developed over centuries in an effort to ensure quality.

This process of gaining access to the collegium begins with graduate education (Tierney & Bensimon, 1996); it continues as one moves into a tenure-track line and further demonstrates expertise in the tenure and promotion process. Assistant professors face limits on what committees they are allowed to serve on and are, for obvious reasons, excluded from input into decisions on the tenure and promotion process. Associate professors face fewer limitations, as their access to decision-making expands after earning tenure and promotion. Only with the earned status of full professor can one be said to have access to the full scope of rights and responsibilities that accompanies collegiality.

The link among tenure, scholarship, and expertise keeps NTTF on the periphery of the collegium. With TTF increasingly focused on scholarship (Bergquist & Pawlak, 2008; Rice, 1986), the faculty member as researcher became the model (Rice, 1986) for the ideal professor, with scholarship rewarded by tenure and promotion. This state of affairs is found particularly at research universities, which place a high value on scholarship, but is also the case to varying degrees in much of the higher education ecosystem. Narrowly defined markers of expertise privilege scholarship over teaching and service. With NTTF lacking access to tenure and promotion, and typically not seen as engaged in scholarship (Kezar & Sam, 2011), the deck is stacked against their access to the collegium and collegiality, and a faculty caste system thrives.

To be clear, it is not necessarily the conditional access to the collegium and collegiality that is the problem. The problem in this case lies in a narrow definition of *expertise*, the absence of any pathway for NTTF to demonstrate this expertise, and thereby the inability to earn access to collegiality over time. The pathway to inclusion in the collegium for TTF seems clear and, at least arguably, has a rationale behind it. In contrast, for NTTF the pathway is nonexistent and the rationale unclear, reflecting the profession's inability to come to terms with a new category of faculty that does not fit the tenure-normative model that has developed in higher education over the last century. Furthermore, this nonexistent pathway for NTTF sets the stage for unequal treatment at a basic human level (e.g., why dedicate time, energy, or consideration to someone whose presence disrupts the norm?) and indicates a significant rift between the conceptualization of the collegium and the reality of academia.

### *NTTF and Collegiality: Why Does It Matter?*

Perhaps this is not as big a problem as we are making it out to be. There is, after all, some evidence that NTTF may not want to be as engaged in their departments or institutions as a robust vision of collegiality for them would imply (Hearn & Deupree, 2013; Kezar, 2013d). Some, given their career stage or other demands on their lives, might well prefer to remain on the collegial periphery, teaching their courses and going home each night. Could we be making too much of this situation?

Perhaps. However, we see the question of conditional, uneven access to collegiality for NTTF as an important problem with implications for both faculty and their institutions. Specifically, we see at least three problematic elements.

## Waste of Human Capital

When NTTF remain on the periphery of the collegium, colleges and universities limit or waste human capital that can help them achieve their missions. As we have noted, NTTF likely have more contact, with more students, in more varied ways (e.g., teaching, advising, program oversight) than their TTF colleagues. Excluding NTTF from meetings and other decision-making spaces means that those who may know students best are not at the table to act as advocates for students and inform the educational mission. There is also some indication that uncollegial environments can limit the instructional effectiveness of NTTF (Kezar, 2013b; Umber, 2014), and collegiality can shape a more positive workplace environment, improving morale, satisfaction, and commitment (Barnes, Agago, & Coombs, 1998; Bode, 1999; Boice, 1992; Rice, Sorcinelli, & Austin, 2000; Tierney & Bensimon, 1996). In short, uneven collegiality for NTTF makes it harder for institutions to fulfill their missions and serve students.

## Exclusion of Diverse Voices

As we have noted, the greatest growth among minoritized faculty (women and faculty of color) is in NTTF (Finkelstein et al., 2016; U.S. Department of Education, National Center for Education Statistics, 2018). Thus, when we exclude NTTF from collegiality and the collegium, we marginalize and exclude the very diversity we claim to seek. NTTF experiences and expertise in general are lost as well as the perspectives of our colleagues from diverse groups.

## Weakening of the Faculty Body

As noted previously, collegiality is not solely about rights—it is also about responsibilities. Excluding NTTF from service opportunities as the tenure-track ranks dwindle and service duties grow only stretches the time and attention of TTF to unsustainable limits. Moreover, the result of this state of affairs may well be a weakening of faculty governance structures, which can and should be partners to administrators as universities and their faculty come increasingly under public scrutiny and attack. It is counterintuitive to exclude NTTF, who could be assets in addressing these challenges.

Ultimately, the exclusion of NTTF from collegial spaces and experiences makes it more difficult for all faculty to engage in their work and for universities to fulfill their missions (Kezar & Maxey, 2015; Maxey & Kezar, 2015). If NTTF as a category of faculty does not fit neatly into the tenure-normative, integrated-professor model around which collegiality is built, then we must be intentional about finding new and more inclusive ways to engage NTTF as colleagues.

## The Purpose of This Book: Building an Inclusive Collegium

When we began this research journey it was evident to us that there is a problem, one that threatens the health of the faculty body and of our colleges and universities. Far less evident was how departments and institutions nurture positive experiences for an increasingly differentiated NTTF body. So, we took up that provost's challenge and sought to learn more about what collegiality looks like when it "works" for NTTF. In this book, we set out to share how "healthy" departments cultivate collegiality for NTTF, with the hope of giving others a sense of the policies, practices, and mind-sets that might help us reshape and create a more inclusive collegium.

In doing so, we take comfort in remembering that the collegium is not merely some abstract concept: It is a space that faculty define and create. Through interactions and conversations, through setting policies and engaging in practices, faculty define the terms of collegiality (Bennett, 1998; Bess, 1992; Gappa et al., 2007). In this sense then, the standards for admission into the collegium, and the associated rights and responsibilities, can be changed, adjusted, and refined by the profession. Hardy (1991) cautions that collegiality is not some natural state but rather "has to be *created*" (p. 137). In this sense, collegiality and the collegium are organic and must be tended, nurtured, and intentionally supported if they are to thrive rather than wither on the vine.

However, as we were finishing this book, we recognized that perhaps simply describing the collegium as organic was not sufficient. After all, it would be possible to continue to shape and nurture the existing collegium, a space that relies on a tenure-normative model built largely around scholarship and thereby excludes NTTF. Clearly, this is not a model we would support. We envision an *inclusive collegium*.

We do so in the same spirit as Stewart and Valian's (2018) call for *An Inclusive Academy*, a book we highly recommend. While Stewart and Valian frame their push for inclusion around engaging minoritized populations, many of the very ideas (e.g., the importance of relationships, providing opportunities for professional growth) we outline are discussed in their book. This alignment seems apropos for at least two reasons. First, NTTF as a group might be seen as minoritized and therefore marginalized relative to the collegium. Second, much of the growth in diversity in higher education in recent years has been in the NTTF ranks, as TTF appointments have not only declined but also failed to keep pace with the growth in diversity among tenured ranks. The need to include faculty and strategies for doing so, whether applied to faculty marginalized due to social identities or employment status, are likely the same.

The observations and recommendations in this book are based on research that began in 2014. Our work took place on two campuses. Research University (RU) is a private, nonunionized, religiously affiliated research university located in the southwestern United States. Master's University (MU) is a large, unionized, public comprehensive university in the western United States. (As with the institutional names, we use pseudonyms to conceal the identities of our participants.) In the first phase of our research, we spoke to 39 NTTF about their varied, limited, and conditional experiences with collegiality at their institutions. In the second phase, we identified 8 healthy departments (1 department in the humanities, social sciences, STEM, and the professions on each campus) where collegiality seemed to work for NTTF (and others). In this second phase, we spoke to 20 NTTF, 21 TTF, 9 department chairs, and 12 administrators (deans, vice presidents, etc.).

Data across the 2 phases of the study gives us perspectives from 101 people and a broad view of NTTF experiences as well as the problems and promise in creating a more collegial culture for NTTF. The characteristics of participants across the 2 phases mirror, roughly, the make-up of the full-time faculty nationally as of 2017 (U.S. Department of Education, National Center for Education Statistics, 2018). Genders were almost evenly balanced (51 women, 49 men, 1 declined to identify), with women perhaps slightly better represented in this study than on the faculty nationally (46%). In terms of racial and ethnic diversity, 24% of NTTF in our study identified as part of a minoritized group (in line with the national figure of 22% for full-time faculty overall), while 29% of our TTF sample identified as part of a minoritized group. In terms of disciplines, 27% of our faculty participants (both TTF and NTTF) were from the humanities, 33% from the professions, 18% from the social sciences, and 22% from STEM.

We offer three points for clarity. First, our focus here is on what others (not necessarily NTTF themselves) can and should do to shape collegial spaces for NTTF. To be sure, NTTF themselves play a significant role in shaping those same spaces and experiences (Haviland et al., 2017). However, the purpose of this book is to discuss what those with more established and secure positions can do to support the integration of NTTF into the collegium, for it is administrators and TTF who typically set and enact policies and practice. Second, while we draw much of our data from recent looks at healthy departments, we do also draw on positive stories from NTTF in the earlier phase of our work. While these faculty might not all have been in departments that met the criteria to be "healthy," their insights (both positive and negative) can nonetheless illuminate what positive collegiality for NTTF can or should look like. Third, our focus here is on "what works" to shape positive collegial experiences for NTTF. With this in mind, we generally draw on the positive examples and stories from our data. However, from time to time, we share negative or counterexamples, to name and illustrate the obstacles higher education faces.

Our primary audience for this book is institutional leaders, department chairs, tenure-line faculty, and leaders in the academic profession. These individuals are central to shaping the experiences of all faculty, including NTTF, as well as shaping professional norms that in turn influence campus and departmental policies, practices, and culture. It is with this primary audience in mind that this book is written. Our driving purpose is to both convey a sense of urgency around doing more to engage NTTF in the core work of the university and outline strategies for doing so. We also think that many of the ideas in this book apply to collegiality for all faculty and staff, not just NTTF. In this sense, we expect and hope readers will use the lessons that follow to shape robust, healthy collegial environments more generally.

We also hope to reach NTTF who are themselves engaged in finding ways to reshape practices related to this population of faculty. These NTTF may become (or perhaps already are) leaders of, advocates for, and partners in the change process required to address the changing structure of the university faculty. Our hope is that the content of this book might be used by these faculty members as well to act as advocates for a more collegial environment for NTTF on university campuses.

## *Overview of This Book*

We have organized the book around several of the big ideas present in Figure 1.1 (interpersonal trust and respect, professional expertise, context). The middle chapters of the book are loosely organized around short-, medium-, and long-term ideas. We begin in chapter 2 with an exploration of how interpersonal trust and respect develops and is nurtured in healthy departments. As Tierney (2008) has noted, personal relationships are central to building the interpersonal trust that undergirds collegiality. Facilitating human interactions and knowing might be the lowest-hanging fruits in terms of building collegial spaces, for while relationships surely have long-term dimensions, the foundations for these relationships are built via small, short-term steps. Everyday interactions, inclusion in social events, and simply being available and pitching in can build positive personal relationships, a sense of shared purpose and mission, and trust. In this chapter, the role of social identities in shaping these interactions is particularly salient.

In chapter 3, we examine ways in which healthy departments foster respect for and formal recognition of the professional expertise of NTTF. Although individual behaviors contribute to the recognition of expertise, professional respect is also enacted or demonstrated through structural means such as policies and practices. This fact means that this dimension of collegiality likely takes more time to shape and develop, making it more of a medium-term endeavor for departments and institutions.

We note again that the concepts of interpersonal trust and respect (chapter 2) and recognition of expertise (chapter 3) are often interrelated, acting in unison to nurture collegiality across faculty members. For instance, relationships that build interpersonal trust and respect can also lead to appreciation for their expertise, which can encourage additional personal or professional interactions, thus bolstering interpersonal trust. This relationship means that, while we have necessarily divided the ideas into chapters, some ideas will appear in both chapters, albeit in different ways.

In chapter 4, we examine context as it relates to shaping collegial spaces for NTTF. Context includes disciplinary values and culture, the history of leadership in the department and at the institution, and even physical space. While context surely shapes the collegial climate, it also can be shaped and influenced over time to foster more collegial interactions. For instance, as we note in the chapter, the gender diversification of one department reflected a changing context that ultimately produced stronger collegial spaces for women in the department. Influencing context is a longer term endeavor, requiring sustained and intentional efforts to influence culture along with an awareness of contextual factors—including disciplinary culture, institutional considerations, and the changing structure of faculty work and roles.

Each of these three chapters (chapters 2 through 4) concludes with recommendations for steps different audiences might take to build or nurture healthy collegial spaces for NTTF. These recommendations are designed to be practical, action-oriented steps that individuals or groups can take, from initiating conversations about collegiality and NTTF expertise to reviewing policies and practices with an eye to being as inclusive to NTTF as possible.

In chapter 5, we return to the model of collegiality in Figure 1.1, revisiting this model in light of the findings reviewed in chapters 2, 3 and 4. An appreciation for practical issues like policies and practices is essential, but so too is a sensitivity to softer issues, such as opportunities to build personal relations and an understanding of the role of context in helping or inhibiting collegiality. We conclude by offering principles we believe are fundamental to departments, institutions, and their leaders who are committed to building inclusive collegiality for NTTF.

As you will be reminded throughout, chairs are a central element in facilitating interpersonal trust and respect, recognizing expertise, and navigating context. They are the ones most likely to recognize the impact of changes in the faculty structure on relationships and productivity, to model behavior, to set and interpret policy, and to guide departmental tone and direction. It is chairs who, through their conversations with faculty, use of meeting time, distribution of resources and recognition, and awareness of NTTF needs and interests, may be best positioned to help faculty make sense of and work within the evolving professoriate. Thus, the critical role of chairs will be evident in these middle chapters.

We end this chapter by noting the broader implications of our work. At the risk of overstating this point, it was our collective sense that the departments we studied were positive collegial spaces for not only NTTF but also faculty in general. While we did not specifically explore questions related to race or ethnicity, gender, sexual orientation, or other important identities, we do address them as they arose in our interviews. Surely not all faculty in the departments were equally or fully satisfied; issues around gender and, to a lesser degree, race and ethnicity, were identified by some participants. And when those issues arose, the onus was unfairly on those from minoritized groups to navigate those issues.

But our sense from interviews and observations was the presence of a general tone of positive regard and healthy working relationships across the departments. Even in the cases where tension around social identities was named, it was typically referenced as problematic but the exception to otherwise collegial spaces. Thus, to the extent that collegiality might feel like a rare or precious resource for faculty in general, we hope that the ideas in the pages that follow can be useful in shaping a more inclusive and positive collegium not just for NTTF, but for all faculty.

# 2

## CULTIVATING INTERPERSONAL TRUST AND RESPECT

*How do we honor and dignify each other? It's not because you're a professor so I need to be kind to you. No, it's not that. It's because of the basic human decency that I think we have for each other.—Ellen, TTF, Research University*

*We can only do so much on an organized level, but in the end it does come down to how people treat each individual.—Sabrina, TTF, Master's University*

The interpersonal interactions and relationships that occur among and between faculty colleagues are key to developing, nurturing, and sustaining collegiality. The departments that demonstrated healthy collegiality for NTTF in our study were environments where colleagues had an awareness of and concern for one another as human beings and came together in a spirit of trust for collaboration toward common goals. In these healthy departments, faculty (including NTTF) felt free and encouraged to interact with one another personally and professionally regardless of rank. NTTF felt seen and acknowledged as individual human beings who contributed to their departments' missions and success.

This chapter focuses on what cultivating interpersonal trust and respect looks like and how individuals, from TTF to institutional administrators, contribute to and participate in a culture of healthy collegiality by building interpersonal relationships. Participants invested in personal and professional relationships, getting to know one another in social and workplace settings and building foundational trust and respect for one another as individuals as a result. These relationships contributed to an ethos of communality, a sense that faculty were, whatever their work, striving to achieve the same core goals for the department and the institution. Community members engaged one another for support and problem-solving, recognized contributions to the common goals, and advocated for one another.

## Investing in Personal and Professional Relationships

In healthy departments, participants invested in personal and professional relationships in a variety of ways. There was a significant human element in this investment in relationships, one reaching beyond professional knowing. The relationships that came from this investment of time and energy contributed to trust between individuals and in the broader department culture. As Amy P., a NTTF at RU, said, "We're all humans first." Melanie, a NTTF at RU, expanded on this idea, pointing to both the personal and professional dimensions of relationships with colleagues by noting that, "I think we trust each other. I think we understand the work we do is really hard and that we have to take care of each other in our work-day life." In these departments, this shared sense of humanity meant faculty made themselves available to one another, invited and included one another, and interacted in ways both sponsored by the department and unsponsored to build positive, collegial relationships.

### *Availability*

In the departments we studied, building positive relationships began with faculty being available to one another. When faculty had access or were available to one another, they had more opportunities to see each other as human beings, with commonalities and shared interests. NTTF in our study linked positive experiences of collegiality to the availability of and access to their colleagues and chairs and often spoke of this availability as an entry point for forging relationships.

Mark, a NTTF at RU, described the ease of interacting with colleagues that came in part from being generally present and available, saying, "We interact in the hall, in meetings, and in social functions and talk about different things, just standing in the door of offices and stuff." The interactions growing from that availability were, Mark said, the building blocks for professional and personal relationships. Many NTTF described feeling a deeper sense of belonging in the department when their colleagues made themselves available to NTTF and noted that less than collegial treatment from other colleagues was mitigated by having access to departmental colleagues who made themselves available.

One of the easiest and most common ways to increase access and availability was by leaving one's office door open. Open doors within hallways and buildings encouraged faculty colleagues to say hello in passing, drop by, have a quick conversation in the doorway, or engage in quick problem-solving in the hallway. Open doors also made faculty members, especially NTTF, feel like it was alright to drop by with a quick question (e.g., to discuss a syllabus) or welcome other colleagues into their office spaces.

NTTF described being more informed about their departments, their rights, and their opportunities when their chairs in particular made themselves available to faculty. They appreciated being able to go to their chairs for support, especially when navigating their positions coupled with their own personal interests. Libby, a NTTF at MU, described a conversation with her chair in which she was able to candidly explain her hopes and goals for her career while acknowledging her role as a lecturer:

> I appreciate that when I set the stage for my interests, and I didn't know what the answer would be, [my chair] was an active listener. . . . I became more informed in terms of what other steps I could take when an opportunity presented itself.

Many NTTF characterized their department chair as someone with whom they could discuss almost any professional or personal topic; some even characterized their chair as a "friend." NTTF in several of the collegial departments also described the deans of their colleges and even the provost and president as being available, to a certain extent, to all faculty. This left the impression on faculty, especially NTTF, that if their administrators were willing to be available to them, then they must be a valued member of the faculty and institution.

## Invitation and Inclusion

More active than merely "being available" is the idea of inviting NTTF into the life of the department and including them in the interpersonal relationships that exist or could develop. Small gestures (e.g., a thoughtful comment in the hallway or an inquiry about a child's health) could be just as meaningful as a conversation about a conference presentation or an invitation to dinner. NTTF pointed to instances when their colleagues invited them to interact as vital moments in their integration into the department.

Invitations and inclusion took on a variety of dimensions. At the individual level, NTTF described invitations to join colleagues for a quick lunch on campus between classes, to serve on a committee, or to attend a sporting event with a group of faculty as examples of times when they were included by individuals or small groups of colleagues. Anthony, a NTTF at RU, provided a vivid example of what such a dynamic looks like, reflecting on his arrival in the department 20 years earlier: "I felt like if I dared to walk down the hallway or dared to walk into the workroom . . . the circle would part and someone would say, 'Come on in.'" More formally, NTTF pointed to invitations to a private dinner at the home of the chair, or to an end-of-year banquet as gestures that made them feel included.

Predictably, the noninvite or withdrawn invitation could be as damaging as the acts of inclusion were helpful. As Karen's quote at the start of chapter 1 indicates, polite interactions were fine, but having never been invited to join her colleagues for lunch over her more than 25-year career made her lower status clear and placed boundaries on any sense of collegiality. Jennifer P. shared that NTTF in her department at MU had once been invited to the department holiday gatherings, but at a certain point stopped receiving the invitation, a shift of which they were keenly aware. Similarly, Kari, a NTTF at RU, recounted a time when a retiring faculty member had invited the department to a celebratory lunch, but had excluded her because of her identity as both a female and a NTTF. Withdrawn invitations or those never issued carried a personal and professional sting.

Being invited to participate in personal and professional relationships was fundamental to feeling a sense of belonging and worth for NTTF within their department. Liam, a NTTF at RU, described the feeling of belonging that developed because his colleagues "simply extended the invitation" to participate in a department committee. Carolyn, a NTTF at MU, ascribed her multiple-decade stay at the institution to the support and encouragement offered by her chair whose literal and symbolic invitations ensured she "never felt like an outsider [or] a low-life lecturer." In one department at MU, the NTTF faculty described the positive impact of the department's decision to grant voting rights to NTTF. Nicole, the chair, said, "I think feeling included, feeling like your opinion matters, that you're a valuable part of [the department], I think makes a big difference." Most notable about this department's collegiality was that NTTF like Teresa (MU) described their voting rights as not only recognition of their expertise (a topic for chapter 3) but also a symbol of "respecting everyone's voice as opposed to just having this hierarchy."

Lilly, a NTTF at RU, pointed to the fact that her chair and TTF colleagues invited her input in hiring decisions as a symbol of inclusion as well: "And so while I don't get an official vote, I think that my comments and feedback within that are valued." Lilly's experience suggests that, for some, even when NTTF could not attend or participate directly, a sincere invitation for input or participation was a meaningful signal of belonging, trust, and respect. Several other NTTF from Lilly's department echoed how meaningful it was to "have a voice" and "to be counted." It was a recognition of their humanity.

## Growing Relationships

The climate of availability, invitation, and inclusion evident in the healthy departments created a space where faculty could have meaningful interactions and build relationships over time. These relationships in turn helped to create a sense of belonging, reduce or eliminate the sense of status and hierarchy that is a core feature of faculty life, and shape a work environment focused on open exchanges and participatory decision-making.

As noted previously, social, unsponsored interactions were rich spaces for faculty to build relationships that fostered interpersonal trust and respect. Many faculty like Mark (NTTF, RU) spoke of the benefits of a simple interaction like getting lunch with a colleague because, "You get a lot more candid insight at lunch than you do in a faculty or committee meeting. . . . People let their guard down more and when you start connecting you get to the real issues." For Mark, and many others, the informality of unsponsored spaces were venues to learn more about colleagues, including nonwork lives, and have honest dialogue about the department. Meals, whether provided by the department or paid for out-of-pocket by faculty, were the setting for not only brainstorming solutions to a department challenge or celebrating a professional accomplishment but also getting to know one another as people with passions and generating project or collaboration ideas.

Events that were sponsored by the department, such as potlucks, brown bags, and professional development sessions, were also important spaces for nurturing relationships and creating a sense of belonging for NTTF. For instance, Joy (NTTF, RU) noted that

> the potluck luncheons, the brown-bag luncheons . . . I think those help to improve trust. I think those relationships during that time in front of one another really [do] develop the basis that you need to have those real cooperative efforts and a truly supportive environment that would be the basis for collegiality.

Faculty in one department at MU also talked about the importance of diversity training in which they had chosen to engage because faculty wanted to ensure they were a strong team of role models for their students and responsive to the diversity in their own faculty ranks. Notably, NTTF from minoritized groups in this department pointed to the training as a signal that their colleagues were responsive to the issue of diversity and willing to engage in challenging conversations. Participants said opportunities in the training to discuss and acknowledge their differences established a tone of appreciation for one another's perspectives. The conversations also raised awareness about their commonalities as a faculty unit and the unique perspectives they contributed to their mission to serve students.

It was in these spaces for interaction and relationship-building that issues of rank, status, and position took a backseat to more human dimensions.

Scott, a department chair at MU, pointed out that relationships among his colleagues had grown out of "friendships that build up over the years. In our department, we're very, very lucky that people don't [socialize] according to rank, they do it according to how long they've known a person and how connected they are." Similarly, Miles, a NTTF at RU, described feeling valued and welcomed because "there's no, sort of, class system when it comes to socializing or getting together or anything like that." Anthony (NTTF, RU) pointed to social spaces as the place "where the distinctions between tenured, tenure-track, lecturer, and everything certainly gets washed away."

Faculty pointed out that the relationships, trust, and respect fostered through ongoing informal and sponsored and unsponsored interactions helped to navigate what could be contentious decision-making processes inherent in academe. Miles (NTTF, RU) said that relationships helped his department transcend moments of disagreement:

> We certainly have our moments in terms of maybe different ideas about our direction, our vision, and what the department's [going to] be about, but the very fact that we can have these discussions and disagreements and still have lunch together, it's good. [It,] surprisingly, works well.

In Miles's example, social spaces such as meals helped to not only build relationships but also heal possible strains and remind department faculty of their shared humanity and mission. Greg A., an administrator at RU, found that healing could begin even before issues arose and spoke of the effectiveness of the tone-setting that was accomplished through prayer at the start of department meetings:

> It's hard to pull out the daggers and start fighting if you start a faculty meeting with a prayer and a devotional. It helps set, I think, the tone for, "Hey, let's figure out how to work through our differences," which was not the case at my prior institution.

Similarly, two different NTTF in the same department at MU spoke of the effectiveness of icebreakers at the start of faculty meetings. Savannah saw these as a way to "find out more about one another." Teresa said icebreakers created

> different ways for us to get to know each other on a really, deeper level. And you know, part of [our] work is that we develop personal insight, that's part of our development as [faculty in our field]. . . . And we're just having a lot of fun getting to know people.

The metaphors faculty used to describe their department culture and their relationships with colleagues varied from family, to friend, to strictly professional coworkers. For example, Felicia, a NTTF at RU, said, "My relationships have really blossomed with some of my colleagues, to the point where it's made me feel. . . that we're family." Other NTTF, like Amy P. (RU), explained, "Some of my friends are people from [this department]. So that's nice, it makes it easier to show up and do our thing. . . we really care about each other." In contrast to these more intimate metaphors, several participants like Leah, a NTTF at RU, who said, "I have an 'allergic reaction' to calling people you're in business with your family," desired clear lines between relationships with colleagues and family.

Still, metaphors point to how chairs and administrators can think about creating opportunities for these interactions and relationships to take place. In our interviews, we heard of some faculty (NTTF and TTF) who wanted to view their role as a job; they would come to work, do their job, and return home. This did not mean they were unfriendly or bad colleagues, but it did mean they did not look to the department as a place for familial or friendly relationships. In this sense, they might be less inclined to participate in more social events (e.g., lunches, happy hours)—although that does not mean they should not be invited!

Rather, departments need to be sure they offer a variety of events where faculty can come together. Previously we distinguished between unsponsored (i.e., organic, spontaneous, faculty-driven) events and department-sponsored events. Sponsored events (e.g., brown-bags, award/celebrations, professional development) clearly linked to the job provide faculty who are more comfortable with strictly professional relationships with opportunities to cultivate interpersonal trust and respect while still maintaining the work-life boundaries with which they are most comfortable. What mattered far more than the metaphor of family, friends, or coworkers were the actual characteristics of the relationships. Were faculty included, did they feel comfortable reaching out to colleagues, did they feel trusted and respected as human beings?

## Social Identities and Relationships

We close this section with a discussion of social identities. While the departments were, on balance, healthy in terms of collegiality for NTTF, that does not mean they were without challenges, nor were they nirvana. Issues of social identity, particularly gender, race, and ethnicity, complicated interpersonal interactions for faculty. Most of the faculty participants who identified as a member of a minoritized population saw their social identity as playing a significant role in how they were received, welcomed, and integrated into their departments. Many described experiencing the same point reflected in the literature: The majority of the gender and racial/ethnic diversity among full-time faculty in their departments came from the ranks of NTTF.

When faculty in general recognized the varied social identities in their departments and were mindful of actual or potential inequities that exist for minoritized faculty, NTTF appreciated those efforts and felt seen, heard, and respected. For instance, many departments at RU in particular had a long-serving core of White male TTF and had only started to diversify in the last 10 to 15 years. Elizabeth A., an administrator at RU, described the efforts of her chair to make sure that committees in charge of planning social gatherings were not made up entirely of women as an important and meaningful effort in her department. Echoing both the role of gender and the importance of colleagues stepping up as allies, Carrie, a NTTF at RU, described a feeling in her department that her colleagues were "aware of gender disparity issues, so they try to work against it."

In contrast, when these identities were not recognized or taken into account, a shadow was cast over otherwise positive personal and professional relationships. As the inverse of the inclusion Elizabeth A. and Carrie described previously, Alyssa, a TTF at RU, explained, "At one point I was on five or six university-wide committees and men in my department weren't on any" because the department wanted committees to reflect a diverse faculty body. In this instance, a perhaps sincere attempt to engage diverse voices of faculty was resulting in substantial service inequity.

Felicia (NTTF, RU) described being an underrepresented minority faculty member as "a blessing and a curse." She acknowledged that her presence in her department benefitted the university in its efforts to demonstrate how it hired and retained diverse faculty, which resulted in her having more leeway to do work that was meaningful to her. However, she explained that her work, interests, and perspective would probably go unrecognized and unappreciated by the institution because of the traditional standards for evaluation and recognition within her discipline and the institution (more on this in chapter 3). She said:

> What is the risk if you try to assert yourself more? . . . I can continue to internalize this sort of oppression and live with this burden of silence like nobody really cares about your perspective on things, or . . . define my role for myself.

Felicia struggled to reconcile the value her identities had for the institution's goals with the fact that the work and contributions that flowed from those identities were not valued or recognized.

The traditional homogeneity (White, male, heterosexual) that often dominates faculty populations also resulted in assumptions that could make navigating the work and culture of academia challenging for minoritized faculty. Leah (NTTF, RU) explained that even in her highly collegial department she experienced discomfort as a woman of color:

> Of all the places I have ever worked or lived or gone to school, this has been the place that has been most unaware of its homogeneity and the presumptions one makes when everybody has been so similar. And it's not just homogenous around religion. It's color and it's denomination and it's gender, and, certainly, it's sexual orientation. There's been so much similarity in the minds who have created systems and practices and processes. So as much as I have loved my experience here, I have never, never felt so uncomfortable with the presumptions of what's the right way to do things.

Some faculty, both NTTF and TTF, described the delicate balance they sought in challenging this homogeneity without straining professional relationships. Teresa (NTTF, MU) said she felt a responsibility to speak up as a representative of not only minoritized faculty in her department but also minoritized students on campus. However, Teresa—along with several other faculty of color (especially women of color)—described the efforts she had to make to also be careful and cautious in how she raised issues related to racial, ethnic, and gender inequities in her department. Teresa said:

> I have to be careful about how I frame things, and sometimes I'm not careful and sometime[s]—most of the time, I try to be. But I do share, I just have to—I feel like I have to be the voice for my community, I have to be.

Carrie (NTTF, RU) shared a story about her colleagues assuming that her research agenda focused on people of color within her subject area when it did not. She pointed out the mistake carefully, making sure not to put anyone down and even laughing it off when she addressed the mistake with colleagues. She explained that because she knew her colleagues, she knew both how the mistake was made (implying her own identity as a faculty of color led to the assumption) and that she trusted her colleagues would not make similar assumptions about her work in the future.

Similarly, Maya, a TTF who began teaching as a NTTF at MU, explained that, despite the relatively high collegiality in her department, she was still cautious in her dealings with colleagues:

> In terms of taking care of the business of the department, I tend to be more careful with what I say, because I think there may be people who don't

listen because I'm a woman of color, and I'm vocal about race, orientation, sexism and all that. So, I'm careful. I'm really careful, because if I say too much, then people will shut down, or take it in a little differently, I think.

Maya's words point to how minoritized faculty felt the need to negotiate homogenous spaces, where their mere presence as well as their words and actions could be disruptive to assumed norms and values.

The role of social identity in shaping relationships in collegial departments highlights the tension among the growing diversity of the faculty, the concentration of this diversity growth in the NTTF ranks, and collegiality. In our study, race, ethnicity, and gender were more salient than other identities such as sexual orientation, religion, and socioeconomic background that also likely matter. The ideal of collegiality might arguably be "easier" to achieve when faculty are less diverse and therefore can make assumptions about shared experiences and values. However, the presence of a faculty that is more diverse along many dimensions makes the collegial ideal even more important to pursue, to ensure all faculty are actively included in the collegium. Healthy departments sought to be explicit about their awareness of social identities, and departments pursuing equity across those dimensions stood out as environments where NTTF could acknowledge that even if the department was not perfect it felt better to be part of a department that was at least trying to remedy social inequities.

## A Tone of Teamwork

The positive relationships that developed through availability, inclusion, and repeated interactions contributed to an overall sense of team and teamwork present in our collegial departments. The stories shared by our participants reflected department cultures that had a sense of team and cohesion, with members working toward shared goals. These cultures, shaped by faculty, department chairs, and administrators together, were defined by faculty pitching in and supporting each other; appreciation and recognition of contributions to the shared mission; and, in the best cases, advocacy for NTTF when needed.

### Pitching In and Shared Contributions

Much like the idea of inclusion, faculty described their healthy departments as places where faculty contributed, pitched in, and helped each other out to achieve shared goals. As Carolyn (NTTF, MU) said in linking a desire to see her colleagues succeed to a larger purpose, "We care about each other's success, and we work for our success. But most importantly, we work for student success and that, to me, is collegiality."

One area in which this sentiment appeared was in course scheduling, where faculty described collegiality as an experience of give-and-take in which personal interests were balanced with departmental interests for the well-being of all. For instance, Willie, a NTTF at MU, described agreeing to teach some classes later at night some semesters so that his colleagues with longer commutes might have more humane schedules. While of course not ideal, he did so both to support his colleagues and with the understanding that there would be other semesters when he had a more agreeable schedule.

Faculty also described their colleagues lending a hand to support each other in very practical, instrumental ways. Mark (NTTF, RU) talked about the ways in which his colleagues helped him problem-solve for new teaching assignments as a new lecturer in the department, "If I needed [materials] or assistance, [they] were always happy to help because their main focus was my success. . . and that takes a huge stress off of new people." The assistance and support Mark received from his colleagues engendered a sense of trust and respect for his colleagues.

At times, the ethos of pitching in could be deeply personal. Joan, a NTTF at RU, shared that her department as a whole stepped up for a colleague at a very difficult time:

> We had a lady here whose husband became quite ill and of course we made visits to her while she was tending to her husband. We never thought he would pull through, that's how ill he was, and we made sure that she and her family had dinner on their table.

This kind of support, far more personal and intimate than help with a syllabus, emerged from the kinds of rich personal relationships and knowledge of each other that faculty developed over time.

At the same time, participants also credited the ethos of teamwork as emerging in part from the tone set by their department chairs in particular. Jennifer S., a NTTF at RU, described her department as having an "atmosphere of team work," resulting from departmental and college leaders who promoted the value of all the programs offered to students regardless of the rank of faculty most heavily involved in those programs. Leah (NTTF, RU) described a similar experience of feeling a sense of team among her colleagues because of an established expectation within the department that, "everyone is equal and that everyone is contributing in important ways."

In many cases, the sense of teamwork and shared contributions emerged from the sense of shared mission Carolyn (NTTF, MU) alluded to at the start of this section. As Janise (NTTF, MU) explained,

> Just like anybody else, each of us wants to have our toys set up just the way we want them. But I think, in general, I would definitely say that all of my colleagues want the best for our students, and I think we are united by this idea that we know that we want our students to be taken care of.

This sense of shared mission, a core component of collegiality, allowed faculty to see something bigger than themselves and their own interests and look past individual differences to achieve larger goals.

## Appreciation and Recognition of Contributions

Just as pitching in was important to building interpersonal trust and respect, so was the fact that NTTF's contributions were both appreciated and recognized. Both TTF and NTTF described departmental cultures where there was an awareness and appreciation of what NTTF contributed. Kari (NTTF, RU) used the metaphor of a sports team to make the following point: "It's like being on a team together: Not everybody plays the same position, but it's helpful if you respect what people get done." Similarly, Willie (NTTF, MU) talked about the importance of "being able to see each other as an equal team member, even though you may be stronger in a certain area than someone else."

While discussing the contributions of faculty members, Taylor, a department chair at MU, noted, "When I say 'faculty,' that includes lecturers," because the department faculty was not divided by rank or role in her eyes. She appreciated the distinct contributions made by different categories of faculty. However, Taylor said, distinguishing those contributions by rank or category did not matter because the contributions were all serving the department and, most importantly, the students. Reflecting a similar sentiment, Jake, a NTTF at RU, said, "I think here people don't care so much about status or degrees they hold. . . . People don't care. People aren't going to flaunt their status or education or whatever. Everyone realizes that everyone else is a valued aspect of the whole."

If acknowledgment of contributions was an important component of building interpersonal trust and respect, so too was *recognition* of these contributions to the shared mission. NTTF spoke of the importance of receiving simple thank-you notes from colleagues after serving on committees, of being invited to the end-of-year banquet and being acknowledged in a speech by colleagues or administrators, or of short announcements in meetings that simply acknowledged an effort or a small contribution.

Elizabeth H., a NTTF at MU, appreciated the opportunity to volunteer for committee work as a way to feel more connected to the life of the institution and pointed to the appreciation she received for her service as meaningful as well:

> I've served on committees every year, I think last year was the most difficult. . . . I was with two tenure-track-faculty, [one] was a bit skeptical, but the other [was] very positive that I was on the committee. At the end they were both very grateful. I always receive thank-you notes from the tenure-track in charge of [the committee].

Elizabeth H. acknowledged that she was not compensated for serving nor required to serve on committees as part of her contract, but the appreciation from the department kept her interested in returning for service.

Melinda, a NTTF at RU, pointed out that appreciation and recognition mitigated some of the challenges of navigating a field as a member of a minoritized faculty population:

> Being a woman in particular in a male-dominated field, I've also realized that often women's ideas can be picked up by men in the group and attributed to them rather than attributed to other women. So I've also tried to concentrate on, when I hear somebody taking over, saying, "Well [she] really had a great point . . ." to reinforce what [my colleague said and to point out that she] brought that contribution, and affirm it.

Amy P. (RU) and Libby (MU), both NTTF, spoke of ways in which the leadership of their departments made specific efforts to appreciate and recognize their needs as faculty and as human beings. Amy P. explained that when a professional development opportunity arose, the chair worked to ensure that all faculty, regardless of rank, were aware of the opportunity. She stressed the importance of this effort at recognition, interpreting it as "that this may be important to you too, we want you to know about it, those kinds of things. Instead of just assuming we wouldn't care." Libby addressed the reality of being in a department with limited resources, "You don't always get your way but I never felt that my needs weren't being addressed. . . . And I really appreciate that."

## Advocacy

In the healthy departments, there were times when TTF and others chose to *advocate* for the interests of their NTTF colleagues. As with pitching in or recognition, advocacy was an optional behavior. However, there were moments when those with more power and influence in the faculty hierarchy worked to protect the interests of their NTTF colleagues, perhaps the ultimate demonstration of interpersonal trust and respect.

At times, advocacy was around very practical matters designed to help the NTTF succeed. For instance, Jim, a department chair at RU, described the intentionality of structuring the schedule of and support for a new NTTF. He ensured that the NTTF had three sections of the same class, to limit the number of class preparations the new faculty member had. Jim also talked about pairing new faculty, including NTTF, with more senior faculty who have taught the same course, so senior colleagues could answer questions, share materials, and provide support for new faculty, including NTTF. Similarly, Scott (chair, MU) shared some of the ways he worked to accommodate all faculty regardless of rank:

> Every semester I send out an e-mail to the entire faculty asking them what would you like to teach, what days would you like to teach, what times? If you have restrictions on days and times, list them. Whether it's childcare, whether it's distance and traveling to campus or something like that, you're teaching somewhere else, just let me know.

He went on to explain, "I try to accommodate lecturers so they're just not teaching lower division classes. That they're teaching a variety of classes, upper division and lower division." Scott saw class scheduling as one of the ways in which he could normalize the sense that lecturers, TTF, and tenured faculty are coequal colleagues.

At other times, advocacy was even more personal and tied to social identities. Both Elizabeth A. (administrator, RU) and Carrie (NTTF, RU) spoke to the importance of advocacy around social identities in their descriptions of how meaningful it was when others recognized the role of gender in shaping their work as faculty members and tried to ensure a more equitable distribution of the workload across genders in the department. Teresa (NTTF, MU) who identified as Latina, spoke of a TTF who advocated for her during her early days as a lecturer:

> There was a Latina, [TTF] at the time, and she really liked me. And nobody ever wanted to mess with her, and I think she kind of cosigned [when I spoke up in meetings]. . . . It was an unspoken thing . . . for the most part, if you work with Latinos we just have our backs. So, she just had my back. She just liked me and talked about me and I was somebody who she had respect for, [so] everyone else had to have respect to a certain extent [for me]. She had a lot of power.

Ellen (TTF, RU) explained what she perceived as part of her responsibility as a tenured faculty member to advocate for and support her minoritized colleagues:

> If I've earned the respect and I also have [the responsibility] that goes with that, then if I don't speak on behalf of those things I see that I don't consider to be just, then shame on me, quite frankly, because then out of that, who is going to be heard? It may not be the people who are being treated the most unjustly that will be heard. Right? So, how can we use our voice in the most impactful way for change around collegiality? And so, I do believe it's a part of not only our responsibility but also of our opportunity. But I also consider it to be a sacred trust.

For faculty in general in healthy departments, advocacy was one of the most active ways that faculty, chairs, and administrators could support their NTTF colleagues. The notion of advocacy will be revisited in chapter 3 from the perspective of policies and practices that can support recognition of NTTF expertise.

## Conclusion

As scholars such as Bess (1992) and Tierney (2008) have noted, personal relationships are a central component of healthy collegial spaces. Early in our research, we were struck by how important seemingly insignificant interactions were for NTTF. For instance, whether a TTF said "hello" to them in the hallway or not or had a brief chat about the weather had an enormous effect on whether NTTF felt valued, appreciated, and gained a sense of belonging. And the importance of the interactions and inclusions grew with the occasion: Could a NTTF comfortably join a hallway conversation, was she invited to lunch, was he invited to the department holiday party—or not?

Inclusion in these social and personal spaces matters. Our participants described the importance of these relationships for building a sense of interpersonal trust and respect. As might be expected, department chairs played a central role in both modeling and facilitating meaningful interpersonal interactions with NTTF (Cipriano, 2011). They modeled behavior and positive interactions, built personal relationships with NTTF, and shaped formal opportunities (events, etc.) where interactions could take place and relationships could grow. At the same time, there was also an important organic nature to the relationships as faculty engaged one another informally.

The interactions and relationships that emerged shaped and benefited from the belief that all in the department (regardless of rank) were contributing to a shared goal. This belief indicated an individual and collective choice to put faith in each other as working toward a common good rather than self-interest. These relationships, in turn, sharpened and were nurtured by an ethos of teamwork, with faculty pitching in for each other, appreciating and recognizing individual contributions, and advocating for each other as individuals as needed.

## Recommendations to Cultivate Interpersonal Trust and Respect

When we started this book, the idea of knowing one's colleagues, of interacting with each other on a personal as well as professional basis, seemed almost too basic and simple to mention. We wondered, "Do we really need to tell people this?" Yet as we waded through our data, with examples good and bad, it became clear that these seemingly mundane interactions and relationships were foundational to collegiality for NTTF. Where informal interactions and knowing thrived, so too did collegiality for NTTF; where they withered, so too did collegiality. Thus, we offer the following recommendations for how administrators, department chairs, and faculty (including NTTF) can contribute to a climate of interpersonal trust and respect. Remember, first and foremost, small gestures go a long way.

### University Administrators

1. Communicate: Ensure communications from institutional offices that concern "faculty" are actually being delivered to all faculty (including NTTF) and that NTTF are invited to campus-wide events such as orientation, convocation, and graduation. In addition, be intentional about naming the importance and relevance of social identities for faculty work and relationships. Encourage faculty to consider who is invited and included, or not, in terms of not only events and activities but also topics of conversation as well as policies and practices.
2. Connect: Work to ensure that dining on campus is highly affordable for all faculty to encourage on-campus meetings and dining among faculty colleagues. (At RU, the institution subsidized the cost of meals for faculty, creating an incentive to gather for lunch in common spaces.)
3. Make yourself available: Open-door policies are not just for chairs. Institute an open-door policy or faculty office hours, or host meetings that include or are exclusively for NTTF.

## Department Chairs

1. Make yourself available: Be proactive in getting to know NTTF just as you would TTF; leave your office door open, walk the halls, drop in just to say hello. If institutional policies demand some meetings or discussions exclude NTTF, schedule regular meetings with NTTF both individually and as a group to ensure needs are being met and voices are being heard.

2. Consider social identities: Be mindful of the role of social identities in shaping the interactions between and among faculty, as well as faculty members' interpretations of their experiences. Be mindful of looking for and then recognizing the contributions of each faculty member, in particular those contributions that might not fit the traditional homogeneous model of faculty.

3. Be a role model: Model inclusion and respect for NTTF. Consider setting the tone of regular meetings in a way that is most appropriate for the institutional or departmental type by including a short item at the start of each meeting agenda (e.g., icebreaker, devotional, prayer, sharing of successes). Encourage NTTF to not merely attend but be part of major departmental/school/college events as presenters, awards recipients, or consultants.

4. Create a variety of spaces for interactions: Provide food at meetings to encourage attendance and conversation between colleagues, or sponsor lunches or coffee dates on campus between colleagues. Orchestrate a variety of socializing opportunities that accommodate different personal preferences and a range of availability schedules (e.g., lunches, happy hours or coffees, dinner conversations). Make sure that NTTF know about and feel welcomed at these opportunities for socializing with other faculty colleagues.

5. Advocate: Be a facilitator and an advocate by being transparent with all faculty and engaging in behaviors that prioritize the personal and professional needs in balance with the needs of the department. Assess committee make-up related to rank, gender, race, ethnicity, and other identities, staying alert for over- and underrepresentation of minoritized individuals. Provide course schedules as early as possible, and consider the scheduling needs of NTTF and TTF equally; scheduling based on some criteria other than rank (e.g., longevity) can signal equitable respect for the faculty as individuals.

## TTF

1. Make yourself available: Leave your office door open whenever possible, or particularly during key times of day when other colleagues

are around. Arrive to meetings a few minutes early to interact with colleagues or make a habit of sticking around for a few minutes after. Volunteer to be a mentor to NTTF. Introduce yourself to new faculty, especially NTTF.

2. Communicate: Send a personal welcome message or reply (individually, not via "Reply All") to general announcements or newsletters that introduce new NTTF. Send notes of congratulations, encouragement, and thanks to any faculty member for an accomplishment or contribution.

3. Invitations: Invite NTTF colleagues out to lunch between classes or for a cup of coffee or tea on campus or off campus. Ask a NTTF to cover a class or be a guest speaker for a class session; offer the same in return. Seek NTTF opinions and ideas on teaching, departmental issues, and scholarship.

4. Collaborate: Reach out to NTTF with similar interests for advice, consultation, or even collaboration on projects while working to ensure such a partnership will not surpass their contractual obligations or limitations or jeopardize their position.

5. Advocate: Talk to NTTF about their needs in terms of support and resources on campus. Speak up about the importance of NTTF voting rights, presence at meetings, invitations to events, and inclusion in departmental communication. Be sensitive to and mindful of opportunities to advocate for NTTF in general, and those from minoritized groups in particular, so that it is not always faculty from the same group (e.g., NTTF, those with shared social identities) advocating for one another. Protect new NTTF time the way the time of junior TTF is often protected by senior faculty. Be open and expressive about any concerns regarding equitable treatment of NTTF, especially if you are fully tenured.

## *NTTF*

1. Express interest in more opportunities, responsibilities, or projects with faculty colleagues and chairs.

2. Seek advice from faculty colleagues, chairs, and deans and stay in the know about institutional opportunities for professional development, compensated service roles, or leadership positions.

3. Ask colleagues out to lunch or coffee.

4. Establish a line of clear communication with chairs and deans (e.g., regular meetings for NTTF, individual consultation, periodic check-ins).

# 3

## RECOGNIZING PROFESSIONAL EXPERTISE

*Getting health insurance, that's terribly important. That makes you feel like you're respected, you're honored. Your expertise is considered important, you're an important part of the entire system. Those are no small things.—Ursula, NTTF, Master's University*

*When you look at someone according to their skill set, there's a lot more opportunity to look at them based upon their position.—Libby, NTTF, Master's University*

As noted in chapter 1, recognition of faculty expertise is typically driven by scholarship. The healthy departments we studied found alternative and more expansive ways to recognize the professional expertise of NTTF—embracing teaching as a marker of expertise, as well as recognizing the professional experience many NTTF brought to academia. Doing so challenged traditional and more limited markers of expertise focused on scholarship. As departments did so, they pursued policies and practices that recognized the expertise NTTF brought to the department.

This chapter shows how these strong collegial departments recognized NTTF as experts, which was an essential aspect of creating a collegial environment for NTTF. These healthy departments acknowledged the expertise of NTTF by valuing teaching as equal to research and recognizing the importance of the experiences NTTF brought that contributed to the shared mission of the institution. They also crafted meaningful work options that included opportunities for scholarship and other opportunities for professional learning and growth. Lastly, the departments recognized the expertise of NTTF by expanding opportunities for full participation in shared governance in accordance with their expertise, one of the hallmarks of faculty work. In short, our departments recognized NTTF as experts and then used policies and practices to act on that recognition. However, navigating these waters was not without its challenges, as the departments confronted a variety of tensions in seeking to recognize NTTF expertise and were limited in what they could do relative to institutional policies that were either silent on or limiting of NTTF engagement. Thus, in this chapter we also highlight these areas of tension and places where the need for progress remains.

As with interpersonal trust and respect, a central actor in facilitating the recognition of NTTF expertise in these departments was the department chair. The chair was a key figure in recognizing, affirming, and creating opportunities for NTTF to display and be recognized for their expertise. The chair played a central role within departments to create a culture of inclusion and respect, including the recognition of professional expertise. As departments worked toward common goals, it was the chair's responsibility to assign individuals to complete tasks, serve in administrative positions, and take on leadership roles. For these healthy departments, rank and status did not drive these decisions; rather, expertise did.

## Recognizing Expertise

The departments that we studied expanded conceptions of expertise beyond the traditional focus on scholarship to include the work in which NTTF were engaged. NTTF were appreciated for their expertise as teachers as well as for their contributions through administrative appointments such as program coordinators for undergraduate majors. Many departments coveted the expertise of NTTF who had industry experience, making them experts regarding the careers that undergraduate students would transition into and the skills needed to do these jobs well.

### Teaching Expertise

In contrast to the typical metrics of scholarly production to affirm expertise, the departments in our study valued teaching, and the work NTTF engaged in around teaching, as a form of expertise that contributed to the goals of the department. With teaching as the main component of NTTF duties and the aspect of their job for which they would be evaluated, healthy departments in our study valued NTTF as experts in their instructional roles, recognizing the value of the function of the role as equal to that of TTF, whose positions involved both research and teaching.

One participant noted that faculty need to be valued for their "flavor," or what they do best. David, a TTF at RU, asserted that part of the "ethos of our culture is those [*research* and *teaching*] are defined as different roles, not greater or lesser. They're functional categories, not qualitative categories." Rather than viewing research versus teaching as a hierarchy, the departments recognized the difference between NTTF and TTF as two different but equally valuable roles that had different functions in the department.

For many of the healthy departments in our study, teaching was recognized as a form of expertise alongside scholarship, and as a result, teaching was valued across the department. Jennifer S. (NTTF, RU) explained,

> I would say that the whole department is committed to teaching, not just the lecturers. And so the department doesn't just value research, it also values teaching. And I feel, during faculty meetings or different times that we're voting on things, our voice is equal to the tenure track or tenured professors.

In this department, both TTF and NTTF taught introductory courses and upper-level courses, because the goal was to have the person with the most expertise teaching a given course rather than separating teaching load by rank. Jennifer S. (NTTF, RU) said, "It doesn't seem like tenured or {TTF} get to teach the fun stuff and then we'll teach the lower-level things." Valuing teaching across all faculty ranks reduced the hierarchy between teaching and scholarship and allowed all faculty to contribute to the health of the department and curriculum for students.

In these healthy departments, NTTF expertise was valued and leveraged for contribution to departmental aims, such as trying to increase the number of students in upper-level courses and encouraging declaring a major within the department. Multiple departments had NTTF teaching upper-level courses because of their skill for teaching. For instance, Jennifer S. (NTTF, RU) said she had the opportunity to teach upper-level courses as well as graduate courses as a NTTF, as did NTTF at MU. Gregory S., explained that as a NTTF at RU, he and fellow NTTF were teaching across the curriculum and in upper-level courses because their teaching skills and respective field expertise were so widely recognized and highly regarded. Anthony (NTTF, RU) said that having NTTF teach upper-level courses was key to recruiting new majors to the department and cited an example of one of his NTTF colleagues:

> Students love [NTTF name], . . . particularly the academically strong students. So they take him for [introductory courses], and they say, "Man, he's passionate and he takes it seriously, and boy, I'm getting a good education. You know what, I might want to major or minor in [field].". . . If they see one of these tenure-track people that they don't know, maybe they look on rate-your-professor or something, but that's all they know about them. . . [If] they look and [NTTF name] is teaching, are they more likely to enroll in it then? . . . It helps the department achieve what it's trying to do. . . . The lecturer enjoys it but it's also helping the department.

Because of this department-wide recognition, each year NTTF were able to choose an upper-level course within their department that they wanted to teach.

Even in the departments where NTTF taught primarily introductory courses, this work was viewed as a benefit to the mission of department. Steven (TTF, RU) explained why teaching among NTTF was so valued. He asserted,

> We, I think, really value the lecturers in that they teach some of our criti-cal, undergraduate classes for our majors. So, we have, I think, a fairly cohesive belief in our mission, in graduate research and also excellence of undergraduate education for our majors. So we place a lot of responsibility on our lecturers to teach some of the core courses and do what we can to support them [to] be successful.

With NTTF teaching most of the undergraduate courses in Steven's department, it was their responsibility to maintain quality instruction. The NTTF were entrusted as experts capable of teaching these courses.

This recognition paved the way for NTTF to be involved in training fellow faculty, including TTF, and to engage in curriculum decision-making. Valuing and acknowledging good teaching meant NTTF were recognized as experts and appreciated for helping the institution (department) meet one of its key goals: educating students.

### Recognition of Expertise Gained Via Training and Experience

Our collegial departments also recognized that the degrees held by NTTF were often commensurate with those of their TTF peers and valued their educational preparation. Beyond these degrees, however, department faculty also valued the expertise of NTTF who had years and at times decades of professional experience.

Though not all NTTF in the study had terminal degrees, the majority (66%) of the participants did, and many departmental colleagues recognized that NTTF had the same training as their TTF colleagues. Carrie (NTTF, RU) explained, "Most people in the department will see you as a colleague and acknowledge that you have the same degree as anyone else, and that you're skilled to teach this, and that you do something good for the department." This recognition of similar training diminished the temptation for placing the expertise of TTF above that of NTTF.

The importance of a terminal degree was clear to those who had a point of comparison. Teresa (NTTF, MU) noted the change in relationships she experienced with TTF when she received a PhD while working at the institution. Through some laughter during her interview, she said, "I'll tell you, when I got my doctorate, I had a totally different relationship with the TTF. Like, 'Oh, I was dumb before and now I'm this bright person?'" Getting a terminal degree meant she felt TTF gave her more credit. Similar to Teresa's early experience, several NTTF did not have terminal degrees in their fields, and this led to them feeling some marginalization.

The seemingly important terminal degree was not the ultimate key to being seen as an expert in all departments, however. In some STEM, professions, and humanities departments, NTTF were regarded as experts because of their long careers in industry. James, a department chair at RU, noted that there were faculty among the NTTF population who had professional experience in the field prior to teaching and that nontraditional pathways to academia generated "considerably more diversity in terms of educational background and perspectives." Benjamin, an administrator at MU, described NTTF as often providing unique opportunities for students because of particular skill sets, professional experiences, or educational perspectives that deepened student learning. In at least some collegial departments, NTTF who held a master's degree and had more than 20 years in their field before coming to the institution were treated as experts with just as much to contribute as faculty with doctorates and 20 or more years of teaching experience.

One way in which multiple departments ensured that NTTF were respected for their industry expertise was to have explicit conversations about the role, rank, and contribution of NTTF. After hiring a couple of NTTF with industry experience, Alyssa (TTF, RU) noted that the department had extensive conversations that included key questions such as:

> How do we treat these people? Because we can't handle the classes that we need to teach, and we need people who are going to be strictly teaching only. And how do we treat them as part of our department, as part of our team, and every bit as important as any other title?

Several participants noted that these conversations were not always comfortable, but they were essential in laying the groundwork for equitable NTTF and TTF interactions.

Like Alyssa's department, other collegial departments engaged in open dialogue about the value NTTF bring to the department, including the industry training and expertise that complements academic TTF expertise. For instance, Teresa, a NTTF at MU, explained that the chair verbally acknowledged and affirmed the work of those with industry experience and their contributions to the department: "They know we work hard so he was, very much, verbally acknowledging our presence and the work we do. And was always highlighting us in the faculty meetings."

Ultimately, healthy collegial departments pushed beyond the traditional marker of scholarship as an indicator of expertise, recognizing effective instruction as both valuable to the department mission and a demonstration of expertise. They also explicitly recognized common educational background as well as extensive professional experience as adding value to the department and to student learning. Department chairs were central in ensuring that open conversations about department goals happened and discussing how NTTF contribute to these goals.

## Professional Growth Opportunities: Reinforcing NTTF Expertise

Beyond simply recognizing expertise, our healthy departments acted on that recognition to engage NTTF in ways that reflected their interests and expertise. Some NTTF in the study intentionally sought their positions because of their love for and interest in teaching or their desire to merge their industry experience with teaching and the preparation of students entering the field. Others were in NTTF roles because of the simple reality of the job market and, reflective of their academic preparation, were hopeful of eventually being able to engage in research in addition to teaching, service, and administrative positions. Across both institutions, departments recognized NTTF's expertise by finding opportunities for professional growth through scholarship, administrative responsibilities, and formal and informal opportunities for professional development.

### Opportunities Beyond Teaching: Scholarship

As a result of institutional mission and NTTF future career goals, many of the NTTF in the study were conducting research, and their workload was unlike the typical teaching-focused load of NTTF. Paul, a NTTF at MU, continued to receive grants and conduct research as a NTTF because of his love for the field and his research interests. He noted that his daily work looked more like a TTF role because he had course releases for administrative work, and he had pursued grants that bought out some of his teaching time. Paul explained, "I've had sabbaticals and I can apply for [institutional grants] and I have remained scholarly. I've published. I currently have that lead article [with professional association], and I've had tons of grad students." For some NTTF, scholarship was an aspect of their role and was rewarded; others were conducting research as side projects because of personal interests; and still others felt pressure to do research because of institutional aims, specifically at RU.

In one department at RU, the department chair tried to align each faculty member's roles with individual interests. The chair acknowledged the equivalent professional preparation of the faculty as a whole, but he was also aware of the nature of the job market and individual interest. Thus he took the position that if NTTF wanted only to teach, that was not a problem; if NTTF wanted to teach and do research, that was not a problem either, and he would work to find course releases for them. The department acknowledged the expertise of NTTF as well as their personal interests and attempted to structure work that fit each faculty member's individual interests on a yearly basis. This was in part possible because the department had autonomy in shaping the roles and responsibilities of the faculty member. While it did not always work out, the chair did his best, and this effort was recognized by NTTF and others.

For this department, the approach to personalize job descriptions per faculty interests worked well, but tensions around the practice existed within the department and in the broader institution. It took dedication by the chair to meet yearly with each faculty member, ask about personal goals and commitments, and then work to craft an individualized experience for each faculty member based on those stated desires. In addition, this approach required balancing the desire to acknowledge expertise among faculty and encourage them to take on grants, research, and administrative positions, with the risk of overworking them or taking advantage of NTTF.

More broadly, as we discuss later in this chapter, unless institutional reward and evaluation structures are aligned to the practice, there is a risk NTTF might feel pressure to conduct research, rather than pursuing it because they are interested. For instance, in a department at RU, conducting research and presenting at a conference was the only way to earn a pay increase. In other departments, the only way to earn a pay increase was through merit pay, and "merit" was tied to publications. Felicia (NTTF, RU) noted that the coin of the realm was research, and if a faculty member wanted to get ahead, then they had to do research:

> Last performance review . . . my chair said, "Oh yeah, you're great! . . . But if you really want to go to the next level [for evaluation ratings], you really need to concentrate more on publishing and your research."

## *Opportunities Beyond Teaching: Administrative Tasks*

In addition to serving on committees, NTTF in the collegial departments had the opportunity to exercise expertise by serving in administrative positions that fulfilled the mission of the department or university. Their roles included running undergraduate programs, leading centers, and facilitating internship programs. Clark, a social sciences department chair at RU, discussed the practice of providing NTTF leadership opportunities that pertained to their area of expertise: "I give my lecturers, in particular, leadership roles in the departments. So my senior lecturer will always be someone who runs my undergraduate programs because they teach the most classes. They have the most contact with the undergraduate students."

One aspect of recognizing expertise was giving NTTF authority over areas in which they had skills, knowledge, and experience. Benjamin (administrator, MU) explained that within his school lecturers have been given assigned time to relieve them from teaching obligations so they could engage in student support services and other administrative roles. He noted that some lecturers had particular skill sets that were valuable for experiences outside the classroom. Bertrand (NTTF, MU) said that his appointment to take on some administrative duties was the result of being seen or known as an expert in the field.

At RU, one NTTF was working on a grant-funded initiative for teaching development for both faculty and graduate students. This leadership position affirmed her role as an expert teacher and gave her the opportunity to share that expertise broadly across the department. At MU, Finwe was leading a grant-funded center with a fellow NTTF. Finwe explained that because of their work, "We're attending more conferences. We've created a class. We've created an archive. We've created a club. And trying to create also, some interdisciplinary connections." For Finwe, this was not just a professional interest. He also remarked, "In maybe a very simple way, it gives also a sense of presence." Engaging in this service work paved the way for him to develop skills and expertise, confirming what we found in our earlier work: that NTTF use these administrative tasks for not only job security but also professional development (Haviland et al., 2017).

## Opportunities for Professional Development

The departments in our study also found meaningful opportunities for NTTF to grow, learn, and be challenged to continue to practice and hone their expertise in the field. A hallmark of collegial departments for NTTF was providing equal opportunities to TTF and NTTF to increase their expertise by encouraging participation in and providing funds for professional development opportunities. Many of the departments provided the same amount of funds for NTTF as they did for TTF professional development. Participants were not only provided with funding but also actively encouraged to participate in opportunities within the institution as well as with external entities.

The encouragement to participate in professional development via funds supported the NTTF in the following ways: It helped them (a) keep a pulse on the current trends and conversations happening within their areas, (b) inform their classroom curriculum, (c) serve their students' needs, and (d) demonstrate their value as equals in the department. For example, Alyssa (TTF, RU) explained that the department encouraged NTTF "to go to conferences, especially about [department] education . . . to work at their craft," including encouraging participation in faculty and teaching development at the institution as well as conferences. Janet, a NTTF at RU, shared that she had received ample resources and encouragement for faculty development, taking a summer sabbatical to study abroad in a program that later directly shaped her classroom curriculum.

At MU, NTTF were eligible to apply for sabbaticals as well as mini-grants for research or creative endeavors. The sabbaticals at MU could be focused on program or instructional improvement, not just scholarship. Multiple NTTF talked about taking advantage of these programs and TTF were advocates in regard to these opportunities. Scott, a department chair at MU, was aware that NTTF were at a disadvantage when applying for sabbaticals because,

> They're teaching machines, they're teaching 15 units. There's that number one [issue]. So being able to come up with a coherent, cohesive research plan that will look good for a sabbatical is more challenging for them than [for] their tenured colleagues.

As a result, Scott was advocating at the institutional level for policy change and was working closely with NTTF, encouraging them to apply for sabbaticals and assisting with the application process.

One of the hallmarks of collegial departments was making the same opportunities or comparable opportunities available to NTTF that were available to TTF. Amy H. (NTTF, RU) explained that she received the same faculty development benefits as her TTF peers. This included a travel stipend that she could use for any form of professional development she saw relevant to her position, not something confined merely to scholarship. Amy H. explained that this benefit allowed her to immerse herself in the field:

> Honestly, for me that is a huge, that's a huge thing. It helps keep me fresh, see what's relevant, keeps [sic] a pulse on the culture. I have so many contacts from when I lived in [city] up there, it helps me keep those relationships fresh.

An added benefit of maintaining these relationships was the opportunity to use her contacts to connect students to job opportunities in the field.

At RU, one department chair was instrumental in shifting professional development resources from TTF to include all full-time faculty. Anthony (NTTF, RU) commented on the benefit of this policy change:

> From the beginning there has been money every year to go to the [conference name], which is probably the biggest meeting. I don't have to present a paper. I can go there just to be exposed to the conversation in the field and other things.

Attending these conferences allowed Anthony to maintain an understanding of the conversations happening in the field and gain further expertise that could inform his work.

In the best cases, chairs worked with their NTTF to honor their professional preparation, skills, and interests by moving beyond teaching into other dimensions of faculty work and providing opportunities for professional growth. Departments found ways to engage NTTF in scholarship as well as administrative leadership, not merely because the work needed to be done (i.e., TTF did not want to do it), but because the work was valued and NTTF had the expertise needed to do it. They also supported professional development more generally.

We close this section on expanded professional growth opportunities with a caution. Helping NTTF who wish to engage in scholarship integrate this into their duties and rewarding them for it is one thing; compelling them to do it when it is not in their job description is another. Similarly, when assigning administrative tasks to NTTF, it is important to ensure that they are given a teaching load reduction in the same way that TTF would receive a reduction. Another caution to note in terms of administrative work is that there is a difference between "letting" NTTF do administrative work because no one else wants to do it and asking NTTF to do the work because it is valued and their expertise in the area is valued. In the collegial departments, NTTF were asked to complete administrative tasks because their expertise brought value to the topic or task at hand rather than because no one else was willing to do the work. Expanding work and roles for NTTF to recognize expertise needs to be done mindfully, and the departments we studied did so. As we note later, alignment between duties and evaluation can be a concern. *Real* recognition of expertise means providing faculty time to do the work, as well as reward and evaluation structures that reflect what is required, expected, valued, and recognized.

## Engagement in Academic Governance: Operationalizing Expertise

As described in chapter 1, NTTF typically have inconsistent and uneven access to participation in academic governance, the core function of the collegium. The departments in our study created opportunities for NTTF to participate in shared governance and departmental and institutional decision-making. Most often NTTF had voting rights, were encouraged to serve on a range of committees and had an equal voice compared to TTF when doing so, and had opportunities for input about the NTTF experience with the institution. The institutions recognized that NTTF should be not only invited into the room but also given an equal seat at the table to contribute to the function of the university. Essential to the opportunity for NTTF to engage in shared governance were institutional policies and practices that encouraged and allowed for this participation.

### Service

Service work drives much of the decision-making and changes within departments and across institutions. NTTF in the study served on a vast array of committees within the department, including curriculum committees, hiring committees, scholarship committees, professional development committees, and institutional committees such as Title IX and faculty senate. Their work was affirmed when they were given the opportunity to serve on committees where their expertise was used and recognized. Again, department chairs influenced and shaped these opportunities, sometimes appointing faculty to committees and other times guiding choices about committee membership more generally. Speaking for NTTF in her department, Carrie (RU) explained that the chair "constantly reiterated that our experience is very relevant for matters related to curriculum and teaching." As a result, the undergraduate studies committee in her department comprised many lecturers.

This pattern was similar across the departments studied. Chairs placed NTTF on committees for which they had areas of expertise. David (TTF, RU) explained how his chair had "been very deliberate about putting structure in place that provide[s] some sense of ownership for lecturers." For example, all lecturers participated on committees and served on curriculum committees within the "areas of their discipline where they did their PhD." Within these disciplinary subcommittees, each NTTF was encouraged to provide expertise and knowledge about the curriculum. The ability to shape the curriculum that NTTF teach within (which we found was a point of contention in our earlier study) was an essential way in which departments visibly valued the expertise of the NTTF, allowed them to shape the student experience, and confirmed NTTF's place in the academic guild.

Engagement of NTTF in department meetings was also a characteristic of the healthy departments. The social science department at MU held its monthly meetings at a time that ensured NTTF could attend if they wished to do so. Kate, a NTTF at RU, explained:

> All of our lecturers in our department are all invited to come to our department faculty meetings; even if you teach one class, you're welcome to come to a faculty meeting and hear what's going on. Everybody gets minutes. Everybody gets the agendas.

It was also important for NTTF to be able to fully participate on institution-wide committees. In our earlier work (Alleman & Haviland, 2016), we found that even when their home departments might not be collegial spaces for NTTF, they sometimes felt their expertise was recognized and valued at the university level.

Again, we offer a caution as it relates to opening up service opportunities for NTTF: Service should not be extra for NTTF, but rather integrated into their roles and duties, with voluntary work minimized and, of course, recognized. On many campuses, the common practice is for NTTF to have a higher teaching load than TTF, with the corresponding practice that NTTF are exempted from service obligations. Indeed, in our healthy departments, department chairs typically took pains to let NTTF know they were *welcome* to serve but, unless they had received assigned time, were also free not to serve and making this choice would not impact their employment status in any way.

### Voting

A central theme throughout our research was that the way in which NTTF felt like their expertise could be exercised and acknowledged by the department was by using their "voices" to vote. The topic of voting was a particularly complicated issue, one filled with tensions and confusion. Institutional policies were typically either silent on or restrictive of NTTF voting rights, resulting in ambiguity and opportunities for departments to interpret policies in their own ways. In less collegial departments, this fact typically resulted in disenfranchisement for NTTF. The more collegial departments searched for ways to empower NTTF via voting.

Voting on departmental issues such as chair, committee service, and other issues was highly variable. For instance, at MU, there was a clear university-wide policy about who could vote for department chair. In some departments at RU, NTTF were able to vote for chair, while they were not in others. Alyssa, a TTF at RU, noted the importance of NTTF voting on chairs: "When we're voting on our new department chair, the lecturers are in there voting, because they've got skin in the game, they need to be part of that conversation." At both institutions, who could vote in other elections (e.g., for committee membership, on curriculum) was typically left up to colleges and departments.

Voice in hiring decisions was also complicated. At MU, NTTF could not be voting members of hiring committees. At both MU and RU, policies, or a lack of clear policies, for NTTF led to ambiguity. As a result, many decisions about NTTF opportunities for service and votes were left to the college or department to interpret. This resulted in confusion about who could vote or serve and when and created unequal NTTF experiences across the university.

Therefore, in the instances when university policies were unclear about voting rights or foreclosed those opportunities for NTTF, chairs of healthy departments often created cultural workarounds that gave NTTF an informal voice as they advocated within the university for an official voice. Lilly's story in chapter 2 of being asked for her informal input on a candidate was an example of a chair seeking NTTF's opinions about TTF hires, even if they were not allowed to vote. While such a workaround seemed to satisfy Lilly (NTTF, RU), others resented the fact that they could participate in the hiring process but were effectively invisible when it came to decision-making. While they may or may not have appreciated the gesture of inclusion, university policies limiting their voting rights in the process were seen as disregarding their expertise.

NTTF who regarded their collegiality experiences as positive pointed to richer engagement in academic governance as an important part of that experience. Although, ideally, policies existed to make their inclusion and participation explicit and consistent, often NTTF engagement came as chairs and TTF sought workarounds to engage NTTF voices, particularly in regard to voting. Although such inclusion can indeed happen at the department and college levels, the importance of engaging NTTF voices in governance, and the need to do so in consistent and intentional ways, points to the need for clear institutional policies that outline NTTF rights of participation. As we noted in chapter 1, we believe the presumption should be one of inclusion, with reasons for exclusion needing to be thought out and justified.

## Recognition and Rewards

In the healthy collegiality departments, there was a public affirmation of expertise, with a message that NTTF were valued, were appreciated, and served a key function in the department. However, like voting, these efforts were complicated by institutional structures that were either silent about or counterproductive for NTTF inclusion. While departments sought to publicly reward NTTF for their accomplishments and displays of expertise, institutional practices around evaluation and pay cast a shadow on their efforts.

### *Awards*

A seemingly small, but important, gesture used by departments was to create formal awards that recognized NTTF for their expertise. This act might include giving out departmental or institutional awards to NTTF who are exceptional teachers. Research institutions in particular are quick to affirm and laud faculty research that is interesting and capable of garnering national attention. Similar efforts were made to affirm the teaching or administrative work being accomplished by NTTF as exhibits of their expertise. These acts could be simple, like listing NTTF accomplishments alongside TTF accomplishments at the end of the semester or in department promotional materials. Clark (department chair, RU) explained:

> We celebrate everyone's successes. We treat each other as colleagues as equals, whether you're a non-tenured faculty member, whether you're a senior professor who's written 30 books, you're going to be treated equally. We will celebrate people's successes regardless of how major or minor they are.

Clark's department hosted a party at the end of the semester off campus, where the faculty and their families could attend and socialize. He went on to explain that at the event:

> We give out awards for everything. We make plaques for all kinds of stuff. You publish a book, you're getting a plaque, you get promoted, you're getting a plaque. They're only $20 gifts that recognize people's accomplishments and they appreciate it.

At the institution level at RU, there has been a push to affirm teaching as expertise as the institution encourages more research. As a result, the institution created multiple teaching awards that are rigorous and open to NTTF. When rewards are created that affirm NTTF expertise, the administrators in the institution and department communicate that this form of expertise, such as teaching, is important.

## Opportunities for Promotion

At both MU and RU, NTTF had opportunities for peer evaluation and advancement, which contributed to some sense of recognition for expertise and professional growth. At MU, the process was more modest than RU and varied by NTTF rank, with the most senior being reviewed every three years and others being reviewed annually. Finwe, a NTTF at MU, explained that the evaluation and promotion process involved both teaching and service. He noted, "Teaching evaluation is part of it, but you're building a portfolio of what have you done otherwise, and elsewhere, and what can you say about yourself that you are a member of the department."

At RU, Melinda (NTTF) explained, "Lecturers and clinical faculty go through a similarish review to the tenure track review, but it looks a little bit different." Like the tenure process, NTTF had to create a portfolio with materials that showed their progress as teachers. The faculty went through a two-year review and a four-year review in which they turned in their binders and gave a presentation before submitting in their fifth year for promotion. Both NTTF and TTF served on review committees for the NTTF going up for advancement. Advancement and promotion for NTTF at both institutions created opportunities for NTTF to present their work to their colleagues and via peer evaluation affirm their expertise as teachers and members of the department who provide and perform essential functions.

## Rewards and Evaluation

As noted, NTTF may have the option to engage in scholarship and in shared governance, but NTTF must also be compensated and evaluated based on metrics that reflect their professional duties and commitments. Faculty evaluation is an opportunity to evaluate, confirm, and certify the expertise of faculty employees. At the institutions we studied, NTTF evaluation was one of the areas where our institutions were the weakest, despite being healthy departments for collegiality overall. This is in part because the NTTF roles and responsibilities at the institution were not consistent, and a uniform evaluation form aligned to work and responsibilities did not necessarily exist.

At RU, NTTF and chairs complained that the criteria for evaluation for NTTF did not reflect the job descriptions of NTTF. The same evaluation form was used for TTF and NTTF. As a result, chairs were seemingly expected to evaluate NTTF on research although it was not an aspect of the NTTF job description. MU did a better job at ensuring that NTTF were evaluated based on their job description and expectations. This was in part because the focus on research was less prevalent and in part because the institution was unionized. The union helped ensure that the evaluation of faculty was directly tied to their jobs. These tensions highlight the importance of considering the ways in which NTTF are evaluated and ensuring that their roles and functions match the metric by which they are being evaluated.

Integral to the conversation about evaluation of and rewards for NTTF is the lack of pay equity between NTTF and TTF: NTTF across the study were not rewarded equally for the expertise they offered the institution. In the departments we studied that were collegial exemplars, multiple NTTF in the study explained how one of the only ways they felt marginalized in their department was that they were not compensated at the same level as their TTF peers. This, they suggested, reflected the institution's value of research over teaching. Adam, a NTTF at MU explained, "socially there is no difference" between NTTF and TTF, but that the biggest difference in collegiality was salary.

At RU, in some departments, merit pay was tied to research for NTTF because it was seen as going above and beyond the job description (as in the example with Felicia), qualifying one for merit pay. This practice created a culture in which NTTF felt as though they had to do more than expected by their job description to receive a pay increase, an interpretation sometimes shared by chairs as well. This problem suggests institutions must identify other metrics that qualify NTTF for merit pay, such as serving as adviser for an undergraduate student group, mentoring students, or earning outstanding teaching evaluations.

We do not pretend this is an easy conversation. NTTF were hired to respond to a rapidly changing higher education system and the need to teach more students in more cost-effective ways. Yet, as NTTF positions continue to morph into key university roles to provide essential teaching functions at the university and fill administrative needs, institutions need to begin to consider how to align pay with expertise. Taylor (chair, MU) confirmed this caution. She noted, "I'm greatly concerned about the tenure-track density problem and the fact that we are relying on lecturers more and more and more to do tenure-track workloads with half the pay." Solutions to this problem might include providing course releases for administrative tasks, like many of the NTTF in our study received. But it should also include seriously considering the pay gap between NTTF and TTF on campus and aligning institutional values and mission with pay structures.

## Seeking Consultation Based on Expertise

What we found throughout our study is that simple gestures by TTF certified the expertise of NTTF in teaching as well as reduced the hierarchy that can exist between NTTF and TTF. For example, Bill (TTF, MU) valued the expertise of NTTF and saw his role as a TTF to support these colleagues. Bill explained,

> The only difference between a lecturer and a tenure-track person is a contract clause. Many have PhDs, many have vastly more experience teaching [subject area] to date than I do. I've taught a lot of [subject area], but I haven't taught in the class in our current crop of students. I don't have any ego or hubris in it. If that's the right term. I treat them as equals.

Across departments that were collegial, TTF and NTTF sought advice from one another about faculty work (i.e., promotional materials, departmental politics, teaching). NTTF across departments noted how they had stepped in to teach a course for a TTF member when they were at a conference, on maternity leave, or had a medical need. TTF also certified the expertise of NTTF by consulting them about areas in which they are experts, especially teaching.

Facilitating opportunities for NTTF to share their experiences provided opportunities to shape institutional policies and practices and affirmed the expertise of the NTTF. At RU, one administrator created a NTTF task force to understand the experiences of NTTF across the school. At the time of our study this task force had only recently begun, but the aim was to understand how NTTF are treated differently across departments and assess necessary policy changes to create a more equitable work environment for NTTF that meets their needs. This task force provided an opportunity for NTTF to utilize their role expertise to make policy recommendations to the institution.

Another way TTF at RU sought to diminish the difference in roles between NTTF and TTF was for faculty to refer to one another by the same title. Amy P. (NTTF, RU) explained, "We call each other in front of students, 'Professor *[name]*,' as far as a teacher title. In that way we very much speak about each other in [/] the same way." When TTF and NTTF were confident in their roles and responsibilities and collegial with one another, the need for hierarchy was diminished and all faculty felt affirmed as they pursued the common goals of the department.

## Conclusion

In these healthy departments, NTTF played essential roles and functions within their departments based on the expertise they brought to the institution. This expertise came through formal training and professional experience.

NTTF displayed expertise via multiple avenues, including teaching in the classroom and engaging in administrative and service functions within the institution. As a result, these healthy departments sought to use both policy and practice to diminish the difference in faculty rank and encouraged full participation of NTTF within their roles, including opportunities to participate in shared governance. Because their expertise was recognized and valued, NTTF were also encouraged to continue to develop and hone their expertise through professional development opportunities equal to those available to TTF.

NTTF in our study were engaged as full participants within the university working toward the institutional mission and promoting learning alongside TTF. At both institutions, healthy collegiality was the result of intentional TTF and department chair efforts to ensure the inclusion of NTTF as full members of the collegium. What was less in evidence but still needed were clear policies at the institutional level that matched this inclusion. Colleges and universities need to elevate the role and function of teaching to that of research at the institutional level. This, in turn, should elevate faculty who span that divide. This shift in appreciation of diversity of roles and functions cannot occur by implementing one or two practices from this book within departments. Rather, cultural shifts need to occur from both the bottom up (within departments) and the top down (within institutional messaging, awards, and policies/structures).

## Recommendations to Recognize Professional Expertise

The recognition of professional expertise is a key component of collegial spaces for NTTF. Broadening the understanding of expertise beyond scholarship, and providing NTTF opportunities to demonstrate that expertise, is critical. So too is being more inclusive in terms of opening the spaces and opportunities typically reserved for TTF. However, for these practices to be something more than workarounds enacted by departments committed to their NTTF colleagues, institutions must play a more active role in terms of crafting policies and guiding practice. For instance, it is not merely a matter of opening governance spaces and growth opportunities to NTTF. Simply giving NTTF the "opportunity" to do more (e.g., scholarship, service, professional development) without ensuring they have the time to do it and are evaluated and rewarded for doing so, is not sufficient. Without institutional guidance, it is likely that collegiality for NTTF will continue to exist only in pockets rather than in the broader institutional and academic culture. Here, we offer recommendations for individuals at a variety of levels for ways to recognize the professional expertise of NTTF.

## University Administrators

1. Facilitate conversations about recognizing NTTF expertise: Honest, open conversations about the presence of NTTF, their role in and contributions to departments and the institution, their academic preparation and diverse skill sets, and how to expand the dominant model for recognizing expertise (typically linked primarily to scholarship) are essential if NTTF are to be engaged as full colleagues. Similarly, there is a need for a conversation about the low pay of NTTF given comparable levels of expertise.

2. Establish clear and consistent policies: Institutions must consider and adopt thoughtful and intentional policies and practices that reflect the consideration of how to include NTTF. Questions that could guide such a process include: What service opportunities should be open to NTTF at all organizational levels across campus? On what issues are NTTF eligible to vote?

3. Protect NTTF from exploitation: Policies and practices should honor the work of NTTF, not take advantage of them as sources of less expensive labor. NTTF should be protected against being compelled to do service without release time, teach units beyond their contractual load for no additional pay, or only earn a merit raise through scholarship (an activity *not* included in their job description). Protection can be enacted through institutional policies and clear messages from administrators that ensure NTTF are opting in when they volunteer, rather than being pressured to do so.

4. Seek NTTF input: NTTF are experts in their own experience. Thus, institutions should engage NTTF in ongoing conversations about their experiences, needs, and aspirations as a way to inform institutional policy and practice development.

5. Invest in and recognize NTTF: Provide an array of professional growth opportunities (e.g., sabbaticals, workshops, conference funding), and create awards and other forms of recognition for NTTF teaching, service, and scholarly contributions. Then be intentional and aggressive in communicating the availability of these opportunities and evaluating and rewarding those who take advantage in ways that are consistent with their job descriptions.

## Department Chairs

1. Include NTTF: Be explicit about inviting NTTF to department meetings and ensure they are invited to speak, especially about matters in which they are experts. Transparency related to voting rights

and NTTF input is crucial. Invite NTTF to serve on committees and take on leadership roles (provided NTTF receive release time to do so) that use their expertise and unique skills. Invite NTTF to lead brown bags, colloquia, and other forums where they might demonstrate and share their expertise.

2. Encourage investment in NTTF: Make sure NTTF know about professional development opportunities, coach them as they apply, and take time to evaluate and give feedback to NTTF in a way that honors the NTTF job description and duties, not the tenure-normative model. Public comments, personal notes, or kind words in the hallway can also be powerful ways to invest in NTTF; encourage others to do the same.

3. Advocate for NTTF: Challenge TTF colleagues who might engage in uncollegial behavior toward NTTF by promoting the expertise that NTTF bring to your department. Be mindful of NTTF service work to ensure that work is divided equitably across all faculty and that NTTF are doing work that is consistent with their role. Similarly, be mindful of interpreting polices regarding service, scholarship, professional development, and so on, with an eye toward collegiality, inclusion, and equity for NTTF.

## TTF

1. Engage NTTF as colleagues: In addition to steps already noted, TTF can recognize NTTF expertise by asking NTTF to cover a class session or guest lecture (an indicator of professional regard), collaborating on curriculum development or research projects, seeking NTTF feedback and ideas related to teaching and scholarship, and sharing course materials openly and collaboratively within the department.

# 4

# UNDERSTANDING INSTITUTIONAL CONTEXT

*Change is really difficult, because culture exists for a purpose, and the purpose is to privilege [TTF]. . . . On the other hand, if you think differently about curriculum, about your department, about role, about how the university can survive, then I think you get to a better point.—Pierre, Administrator, Master's University*

*We are an echo chamber. And if we keep telling ourselves the emphasis on scholarship and research means we don't care about teaching, then that's what'll happen. . . . The notion that they are separate and unequal, and that those who teach are exploited, and those who do scholarship and research are privileged is one of the worst, misinformed, and just bad elements of our culture. And I think we use it at times to make ourselves better, or to keep others out. It ought to be challenged. . . . It's our responsibility to do so.—Jacob, Administrator, Research University*

Recently, one of us was talking to an amateur arborist friend about a landscaping strategy for their yard. Planning for seasonal plantings was the goal of the conversation. However, when the acquaintance was asked, "What is the best time to plant a tree?" his wry response was, "Forty years ago." However unhelpful this quip was for that context, the insight is as undeniable when applied to trees as when applied by analogy to collegial departments. Just as the maturation of a tree reflects the combination of time and environmental conditions, so also the condition of collegiality reflects the history and context of the academic department under consideration.

The aim of this chapter is to place in perspective the guidance of the prior two chapters that focused on *interpersonal trust and respect* and *recognized expertise* by describing the specific factors that make up the context within which collegiality exists and is pursued. In this sense of accumulated condition, chapter 4 focuses on long-term collegiality considerations, in complement with the short-term focus of chapter 2 and medium-range focus of chapter 3. Our subtext here is that collegiality is shaped by more than current personnel, perceptions, behaviors, policies, and resources, although all of these matter a great deal. Like a tree, collegiality exists in both present and historical contexts, and attending to its health requires recognition of the effects of the past and what is required for health and flourishing in the years to come.

## Two Departmental Vignettes

We begin with two departmental vignettes that set forth, with richness, the complicated background factors that shape departmental life. Nested within these brief case descriptions are five formative factors albeit in different ways and to different degrees that contribute to the collegiality in any department,

1. Field/discipline orientation
2. Institutional context
3. Departmental history
4. Chair leadership history
5. Spatial, material, and financial resources

Watch for these categories in the following narratives. Afterward, we will explore the factors more fully and then present a model of interactive functioning that can be applied to various contexts.

### STEM Department at RU

STEM Department at RU occupies two wings and several floors of a building shared with a related department. Faculty offices for the unit, once confined to a single area, have grown into the second wing as subspecialties have developed over time, resulting in bifurcated faculty spaces and some social clumping by convenience. Offices are assigned officially on an "as-available" basis, meaning that as new faculty are hired they are placed where spaces are open and not based on seniority or rank. This ad-hoc process reflects a generally egalitarian bend, in some cases increasing interaction across ranks.

Over the past several decades the department's focus has been shifting toward graduate education and research productivity reflective of departmental and institutional aspirations. The growth in graduate programs and hiring indicative of this research emphasis places an increased teaching load on NTTF. Although this sort of transition in some departments would lead to a sense that NTTF are not doing work that is valued, STEM Department has a strong culture of collegial respect for the contributions of NTTF that is rooted in a history of several long-serving and well-respected

NTTF who were hired after extensive professional careers. As noted in chapter 3, Alyssa (TTF, RU) reflected on faculty conversations within the department about how NTTF are "every bit as important as any other title" and should be regarded and valued with an emphasis on how to treat them as part of the team.

Alyssa noted that the recognized expertise of NTTF had been buttressed by a departmental tradition of strong undergraduate instruction valued among the tenure system and NTTF alike. Together, the professional field experiences and the shared value of teaching as a prized skill have contributed to an expectation that all faculty members are treated with respect. This culture has resulted in hiring expectations in which collegiality and fit with the larger institutional mission are deliberately vetted, to the extent possible. Steven, a TTF in STEM Department at RU, described the department as "fortunate to be able to avoid hiring a disruptor," acknowledging that predicting those tendencies in new hires is difficult. Nevertheless, hiring for collegiality was a purposeful goal: "We've had explicit discussions about that, in fact have rejected some otherwise . . . good-looking candidates on paper because of concerns about they're [*sic*] being a prima donna."

The recent growth in faculty numbers has caused decision-making, which used to be made informally and by consensus, to shift increasingly into a distributed model in which committees and representation are the emerging norm. Although this new structure has been an adjustment in terms of mass participation, NTTF have equal representation and say on departmental committees, excluding the hiring of tenure system faculty based on university policy.

Nevertheless, STEM Department is experiencing a transition that its members will have to navigate for collegiality to be maintained as a central feature of faculty life. The expansion of the department in general has inevitably reduced interpersonal knowing and increased use of representative leadership, which makes for a different sort of departmental experience. Turnover in the chair role in recent years has led to concerns about what is needed for effective and consistent departmental leadership. A few participants expressed concern that the increased emphasis on graduate instruction and research could further reduce the commonality of experience of teaching undergraduates and the conversations across employment types that result. Similarly, participants were aware how a departmental and institutional emphasis on research might put pressure on hiring decisions, even on NTTF hiring, to bring in those whose preparation and experience is strong on scholarship but weaker on instruction. Finally, although not a central theme, concerns about women's voices in a traditionally male-dominated discipline was an undercurrent raised by several participants, who felt that this diversity, although valued, could destabilize a collegiality of homogeneity that was easier to maintain in a different era.

Nevertheless, participants pointed to a number of resources in STEM Department that provide shared energy and focus for an increasingly diversified unit. Many participants identified the religious identity and mission of the institution as a factor that is collectively motivating, in terms of serving students and engaging colleagues with respect and care. Faculty members discussed the importance of inclusive processes, regardless of the organizational model of decision-making. Additionally, a number of annual nonacademic student/faculty events are part of the departmental calendar that bring everyone together and provide new contexts for appreciating others. Finally, departmental members have a shared sense that collegiality is a departmental value that must be pursued and nurtured over time. On this front Jennifer S., a NTTF in STEM Department, reflected:

> I definitely see how the tenured professors or the senior lecturers have really made an effort to mentor and include and help the newer faculty members, and so I feel like that's a really big deal about the environment in the department. And so even faculty who were very research focused, I still feel like I could go ask them questions, they're still, that my development or my questions or things are still important to them. So, yeah I feel like collegiality isn't something that just happens by accident.

The collective awareness that collegiality requires deliberate tending may be one of the most important resources for STEM Department in changing times.

### Social Science Department at MU

Social Science Department at MU is located in a large building it shares with several other departments. The combination of multiple departments and churn of membership have made it challenging to keep up with new faces, potentially reducing the sense that one is known and knows others meaningfully. Despite the challenges of office distribution and space, the chair expressed how important it was that the department has remained in a single building, unlike others that have been divided across structures as growth requires:

> It's a sense of space. You see each other, physically see each other. You feel more part of it because, look, let's be honest, if anybody was going to be outside of this particular building, which is where most of our faculty [are]

housed . . . it would be lecturers and then they would feel that much more distant from the department.

With space at a premium, office sharing is required regardless of rank, with exceptions for those with heavy student advising loads. Although the institutional expectation is that each professor has their own desk, that desk may be in a room with one or two others. Consequently, faculty members are left with difficult choices: work in a potentially distracting office environment with colleagues, work out an alternating use schedule, or simply work elsewhere. Chris, a TTF in Social Science Department, articulated the opportunities and liabilities of this arrangement, and how one chair attempted to ameliorate the effects:

> That was one of the things an earlier chair did, [he] tried to get everybody on a three-day-a-week schedule, just to make sure that people were around and interacting more. But I do think it is a barrier, [my office partner] and I are very good friends and we've been friends for a long time, so we're happy to be in the same space, but we also both can't get as much work done, so I think that's an issue.

For those with explicit research responsibilities, the discipline's culture of solo authorship tends to further pressurize expectations of a quiet work space and reduce the desirability of collegial interaction on professional scholarly tasks, though some participants described working collaboratively despite this norm. For some long-serving full-time faculty, space issues exacerbate rank issues: hierarchical tendencies, fed by the department's history of hiring its own master's students as lecturers, have been aggravated through requirements of office sharing that sometimes pair senior faculty and NTTF.

The turnover of part-time faculty positions has also made challenging an important sign of departmental inclusion: the structuring of mailbox assignments. Departmental mailboxes are divided between TTF and NTTF, ostensibly because the latter changes frequently and the former does not. But for those full-time NTTF who are long-standing members of the department, the functional inconvenience of needing to refind one's mailbox each year as part-time faculty change provides a symbolic message of one's perceived impermanence. In a similar way, frequent turnover means that some other departments at MU only provide name cards for office doors for tenure system faculty and exclude lecturers from office photo boards. By contrast, in Social Science Department, each faculty member receives a permanent name card and is included among the department faculty photographs. These small organizational decisions are important signaling mechanisms for those who perceive they are on the margins already.

In part, the office and mailbox situations reflect elements of MU's institutional geography, identity, and mission. MU's location near a major metropolitan area with major research universities nearby facilitates the hiring of *freeway flyers*, a term frequently invoked by participants to describe faculty who hold teaching appointments at a number of institutions simultaneously. The public, student-focused mission has resulted in a student body less familiar with navigating college, requiring a higher level of support by faculty members. This at times has brought to the fore competing institutional expectations, such as MU's increasing scholarly aspirations that may conflict with a student-focused mission. The confluence of these factors clearly strains physical, material, and human resources, even as faculty capitalize on the opportunities of their metropolitan setting and public mission.

Although it might seem that Social Science Department has a number of factors that militate against collegiality, the unit has blossomed in this regard over the past several decades, in part through the efforts of a string of departmental chairs who made a priority of developing a positive environment for all faculty. In an earlier period chairs were described as "detached" and not interested in the integration of NTTF. Low morale pervaded the department. Chris (TTF, Social Science, MU) recalled the slow work of culture change:

> We had a department chair who was very effective at getting buy-in into a departmental culture from people who had either gotten discouraged and embittered, or who had felt marginalized, and who had lots of good strategies for involving them. I think what [the chair] did was [enlist] them in conversations about what to do with various curricular matters, for example, and asked them to participate in particular committees that were a bit involved, ad-hoc committees, or committees that were dependent upon appointments by the chair.

The important successes of this chair were capitalized on by succeeding generations of departmental leadership through a combination of equity, fairness, and respect for the contributions of all faculty. An additional source of respect for NTTF may have resulted from the instructional role of lecturers who, years ago, ably taught several core classes that made them important to the department and recognized as experts.

The outcome, over time, is a department where NTTF are expected to contribute meaningfully in the classroom and in departmental governance, which sometimes surprised new hires, such as Gagarin (TTF, Social Science, MU):

> Well, first thing I noticed when I came to faculty meetings here . . . all of these people speaking up—that this is a much larger department—I

just assumed were the tenured faculty and I subsequently found out that
they were lecturers. And that really surprised me because where I came
from before lecturers were never participants in faculty meetings—much
smaller department—but they were excluded from any kind of say over
what classes they would teach, the management of the department, the
sitting on committees in the department. Here, lecturers are offered the
opportunity to do that and it's made clear that they don't have to, that,
[not participating] won't prejudice their standing within the department
if they don't.

This accumulating sense of collegiality is not one free of difficulty. State
budget cuts and collective bargaining at various points have strained relationships between TTF and lecturers. Even now, one participant suggested
that collegiality may be on the wane under new departmental leadership that
is less attentive to the equitable distribution of resources and input. As Social
Science Department continues to grow and experience leadership change,
drawing on this history of collegiality despite challenges of institutional and
geographic environment, resource deficiencies, and personnel turnover is
vital to the future health of the department.

## The Five Factors Explored

In the discussion that follows, we dive into each of the five contextual factors
(field/discipline culture; institutional context; departmental history; departmental leadership history; and spatial, material, and financial resources) and
explore the nuance within each that arose across our eight collegial departments. Understanding the substance of these five factors is a worthwhile step
toward diagnosing and responding to contextual factors that impede collegiality. Throughout, we refer back to the two vignettes to highlight the variable
and nonlinear nature of collegiality over time and context.

### Field/Discipline Culture

As Tony Becher (1989) highlighted in his book *Academic Tribes and
Territories,* each field or discipline (*field* being a professional or practical academic area; *discipline* includes areas with native theoretical content) contains
distinctive cultures, practices, and focal concerns that alternatively tend to
require or tend to resist activities that promote collegiality. On a continuum,
mathematics, history, and some natural sciences—which require intensive
lab work and where the availability of graduate students for teaching and
advising may reduce the need for colleagues to pitch in—might tend toward
singular work, isolating and competitive. Performing arts tend to be highly

collaborative, requiring various technical subspecialties to pull off a perfor-mance. As one of our participants put it: "I think the bigger thing is that this is just the way theater happens. Theater is a collaborative thing and if you want to go solo you're going to be in trouble." Education, social work, and other "helping" professions might naturally tend toward supportive environ-ments even as work is sometimes done in isolation from others. Through graduate socialization and departmental experience, the expected nature of the work within any field or discipline is reinforced over time.

Nevertheless, fields and disciplines are not monoliths, particularly in their departmental manifestations. The hybridization and cross-fertilization of academic areas may increase collaboration where traditionally there has been little. Institutional cross-disciplinary initiatives, such as teacher prepa-ration in STEM, or simply deliberate scholarly collaboration on a book or new course creation, as we saw with Social Science Department, can disrupt departmental norms. Specialization can also have differential effects. As a department chair, Jim (STEM, RU) noted how colleagues tend to clump by interest around subdisciplinary specialization, increasing subgroup cohesion but reducing department-wide interaction somewhat. By contrast, Amy H., a NTTF at RU, argued that individual specialization in theater makes col-laboration necessary and possible:

> We're here to make beautiful things happen on stage and to teach how to make that happen. We all have such individual roles that we play . . . Nobody does the exact [same] job here. Where in English you could have like three composition teachers . . . or math you could have five people teaching calculus because you have that many students . . . you're doing the exact same thing . . . . Each of us has our own specialty.

By contrast, a professor in one of those departments where multiple individu-als teach the same courses argued that this similarity of content and resulting sequencing through his program also made collaboration vital: "We have mul-tiple sections of the same course, so we have agreements that are jointly decided communal agreements about where we all have to stop." As these seeming counterexamples highlight, collegiality serves improved outcomes at different points of this field/discipline continuum, though perhaps for different reasons.

Yet some disciplinary cultures contain tendencies of membership and participation that, while having nothing to do with the content of the work explicitly, continue to influence both the diversity of membership and the type of participation. This may be the case particularly in STEM areas that historically have been strongly gendered. Lilly, who was the first woman in her department, commented on the challenge of her dual roles, which con-tributed to her departmental marginality and experience:

I still, coming in as a lecturer, and I was very young coming in as a lecturer, the department was very male and very old. That was very intimidating coming in as a young woman. . . . [The established faculty] were all teaching classes, of course this was before [RU], our department got big, so there were smaller classes, and so I believe that just by nature they didn't really like any lecturers because they thought it was silly for [RU] to even have that type of position. So, there was a little concern there and what I did was I came in and kept my mouth shut for a long time.

The confluence of gender and role within a particular historic moment in a department accustomed to homogeneity led to Lilly's self-silencing, at least for a time. Lilly was quick to note that her chair was supportive of her presence and voice, and gradually she gained the appreciation and respect of her colleagues as she was given opportunities to demonstrate expertise through teaching (including winning a major institutional teaching award) and administration (serving as undergraduate program director). She also noted that when she had a maternity emergency, she was supported by her male colleagues. Thus, although field and disciplinary orientations, such as a history of primarily male faculty, may establish general patterns of membership and relating, specific individuals and units may redefine belonging and regard in such ways that promotes an overall collegial environment for NTTF.

## Institutional Context

The geographic location, control, size, history, mission, culture, leadership, resources, and other broader institutional factors play an important formative role in departmental collegiality in ways that may seem invisibly normal to long-time faculty. Often departments are in a reactive position, explicitly or implicitly required to respond and align with institution-level initiatives, expectations, and purposes. Yet the history and culture of a given department give it a trajectory that may make such alignment natural or difficult, such as a humanities department seeking its place in an increasingly grant-oriented research institution. The accumulation of departmental perceptions and responses to this institutional context shapes the collegial culture of the department over time. Although the possible effects are legion, here we focus on two: a shared institutional mission that attracts individuals to a college and shifts in institutional focus over time that require the adjustment of individuals and departments.

### Shared Institutional Mission
Although some individuals are pleased to accept a faculty role wherever one may be available, professors often at least desire employment at those

institutions where they have a sense of mission alignment (Gappa, Austin, & Trice, 2007). This was certainly the case for our two study sites. At MU, some participants found the public, student-focused mission created a compelling environment where teaching and learning were valued. At RU, the religious identity of the institution drew faculty who wanted to align ideologically with their employer and feel the freedom to integrate personal religious belief more freely and openly with their professional work.

In both cases, institutional mission connected at least indirectly to departmental collegiality. Andrew, a NTTF in a humanities department at RU, spelled this out, asserting:

> Especially at a Christian institution, where I think collegiality also has a definite aspect to it of forgiveness and trying to remember that the people you work with are brothers and sisters in Christ . . . [that] all of us are works in progress, and letting things go, not holding grudges. Not turning things toxic.

Similarly, at MU the shared student-centered focus provided a point of solidarity and shared purpose that enabled individuals to bracket behavior or policies that might have been viewed negatively otherwise.

The attraction of faculty to the institutional mission fostered communities of support. For instance, Lilly (NTTF, RU) described a situation when a colleague's child faced a terminal illness. The department circulated a list of needs, which were quickly met. Lilly suggested that collegiality is easier in an environment where people care about one another's lives and, in this case, that caring was buttressed by shared religious commitments. The rub, Andrew (NTTF, RU) suggested, was that institution-level mission could create expectations for policy and behavior that, if not met, could actually increase frustration and disenchantment because stakeholders place value and expectation on the harmony between purpose and practice. For example, at an access-focused institution, cuts to student aid or support may elicit a particularly strong response as a decision that appears to counter stated community aims. The relative potency and ubiquity of institutional mission can function as an impetus to departmental collegiality, or it can intensify discontent if beliefs do not align with policy and behavior.

## Shifts in Institutional Focus

Over time, changing institutional expectations and aspirations, such as toward a research focus, can shape departmental membership; expectations; and, indirectly, the environment of collegiality. The specter of research productivity, an element of the institutional identity equation at many colleges and universities, loomed particularly large at RU but was present at MU as well. The case example of STEM Department highlights the realities of resource allocation toward hiring nationally visible researchers as well as the concerns held by existing faculty as to the implications of this trend for the perceived role of NTTF. At both institutions a subset of senior faculty, mostly tenured, were hired before research expectations become normative. Dana, an administrator at MU, reflected on the faculty lifestyle some of them continued to enjoy for decades that shaped their expectations of faculty life and membership:

> It was a life, let me tell you. And these guys were all World War II vets, very nice men. But it wasn't a time when [MU] was requiring scholarship of faculty when they were hired. They didn't do research. They came. They taught their classes. They were great teachers. But they were also of the ilk, "I'm going to come in and I'm going to do my 8:00 to noon. And don't bother me." And so, collegiality was a very different. You either were in the men's club or you weren't. Lecturers weren't in the men's club. It was all tenured faculty.

In this example, one echoed at RU, the persistence of a department subculture over time was increasingly dissonant with the culture of the institution and even the field or discipline, in terms of both engagement with scholarship and engagement with NTTF. The easy solidarity of shared life experiences and professional expectations simply did not fit with an increasingly and necessarily diverse faculty membership, and refusal to participate in professional rituals (e.g., service, meetings) meant that bonds were not formed with newer faculty. By contrast, professions departments on both campuses in our study were confronting changes to structure and membership related to online and distance education. Rather than further entrenching, the chair of the professions department at RU recounted internal conversations of how to maintain the "family" feel of the unit even during and after transition to new technologically driven delivery formats.

## Departmental History

As the story of the World War II veteran faculty illustrates, the history of the department, specifically in the past 15 to 30 years, represents a kind of "biography" and "family history" that current departmental members live within, and over time, reinforce or modify. This history contains collegiality-shaping factors, such as number of faculty, demographics (e.g., distribution among age, race, gender, and other identity categories), employment roles and expectations (e.g., long-tenured faculty who primarily teach), subspecialty distribution (e.g., types of political scientists), and ingrained shared practices or cultural expectations (e.g., monthly departmental brown bag lunches).

As both case examples illustrate, faculty longevity in particular is a potent ingredient of the collegiality of a department, establishing extensive interpersonal knowing that can result in a closed "old boy's network" or a tradition of inclusiveness and shared concern. As such, the forms and effects of this longevity are various. Long-standing departmental norms that full professors do not participate in service, such as outreach to new students, can create divisions that saddle NTTF with such responsibilities, often outside their contractual obligations (Haviland, et al., 2017). Long gaps between new hires may mean that official practices, such as new faculty mentoring, are not well codified or observed. Efforts to hire and include faculty from historically underrepresented groups in departments with little experience at doing so may mean that engrained culture, invisible to long-serving members, is not experienced as welcoming by others (Turner & Myers Jr., 2000). Theo, a NTTF in a social sciences department at RU linked this struggle to a lack of institutional expectations as to what collegiality at the departmental level entails:

> Departments create their own normative structures, which are deeply rooted in the traditions that go back decades of time. So unfortunately, this related to the notion of tradition, within some departments the tradition has been really kind of patriarchal, and I can understand how not only being a lecturer but being a woman here could be a pretty ugly experience on a number of levels. And so that's what happens with departments trying to guide themselves and have a tradition of being mostly led by men and men with a certain kind of perspective. It could be pretty unwelcoming to faculty members who are women.

A number of NTTF women in our study noted that culture change had happened in their male-dominated departments, but often primarily as a result of retirements and shifting departmental membership, rather than a change in the approach or attitude of those faculty long employed.

Nevertheless, longevity can serve to benefit NTTF collegiality under the right conditions. In both case examples, the departmental focus on quality undergraduate instruction, often through gatekeeper courses recognized as important for subsequent upper-level course success, offered NTTF opportunities to establish departmental credibility and recognized expertise. Additionally, departments in the professions or those with a clear professional pathway have the advantage of hiring individuals with respected field experience to teach courses, capitalizing on professional expertise and network connections. However, departments that have few full-time NTTF may find that the lack of established expectations for inclusion requires deliberate adjustments of attitude, policy, and behavior, such as recognizing that heavy teaching loads might preclude participation in previously established lunches, department meetings, and professional development opportunities. As noted in chapter 3, several of our healthy departments were intentional in talking with faculty about the nature of NTTF work and roles, as well as ways to integrate them into the department.

A second major element of departmental history prominent in our case institutions is the way that change in membership, both size and make-up, alters climate, requiring adjustments. Organizationally, an increase in the size of a department's faculty can require new decision-making structures, such as in STEM Department, which may shift practice toward a representative model and away from consensus. Felicia (NTTF, RU) noted how adding new and more diverse professors shifted the power dynamics away from several contentious senior faculty members: "The department has grown, now their influence is still felt, but now that you have more voices or different perspectives and you have the feminine perspective being more vocal, that has changed the way people view contributions in general." Kari (NTTF, RU) also described how the hiring of several young TTF created a new social center that was inclusive of women and NTTF in a way that had not previously been the case.

These shifts and changes, although primarily positive in the given examples, do not suggest inevitable or linear progress toward collegiality. Hiring faculty who do not share collegial norms and values, for instance, might disrupt a trend of positive collegiality in the department. Departments each have their own unique legacy of tendencies, positive and negative, that emerge, often in moments of political tension, resource scarcity, or curricular reform, to require fresh attention. In many cases, these situations stem from failures of leadership, a topic to which we turn next, that have set in motion tendencies of climate and culture that are most damaging to those with the least amount of power.

## Departmental Leadership History

Chairs represent one of the single most influential factors in shaping departmental culture, climate, and collegiality (Kezar, 2013d). Relevant aspects of a chair's background and tenure include longevity in the department and in the role, status as an institutional insider or outsider (often related to whether the chair was an internal hire or not), and leadership approach and style (e.g., relatability, accessibility, tendencies toward structural, interpersonal, political, or symbolic thinking). Although particular chairs may have a disproportionate influence on a department positively or negatively, as the case of Social Science Department at MU shows, it is often the accumulation of influence resulting from a series of chairs over time that results in the specific condition and quality of departmental collegiality.

Michael, a chair in the professions department at RU, highlighted this point, describing several decades of strong female leaders leading up to one particularly important chair and what that meant for the sense of inclusion of NTTF and faculty in general:

> Part of it was being a woman in leadership and desiring a structure reflective of her values and ways of knowing and being in the world as a woman who had not always been valued and respected. She was trying to create something different as a woman in leadership, but also as a [professional in the field]. She felt like all voices matter. Her faith played a role. Her professional identity played a role, and her gender played a role. I think for those of us who have followed her, we've learned those same values, and cherish those same attributes of the culture.

From Michael's comments, the accumulated effect on departmental culture as an inclusive space is clear, but this outcome took time to develop and reinforce.

Because of the importance of the sometimes nonlinear and accumulating effect of departmental leadership history, the role and task of a given chair related to collegiality may already be considerably determined, or at least directed, toward preexisting issues left untended by the predecessor, including differences of personality, ideological perspectives, or gaps in policy or practice. Benjamin (administrator, MU) described the history of animosity between faculty in one of his units and the difficult work required to rectify those rifts. Scott, a department chair at MU, reflected on his process of preparing for the central collegial challenges that awaited him:

> So [before] I took over as chair . . . I was also anticipating what I was going to do when I took over. My priorities were basically to create a better sense of camaraderie and collegiality in the department and morale in the department, but also to repair the relationship with the Dean's office.

History and context may shape the task, but the selection of a chair also sets a course toward, or away from, an inclusive collegial environment. For this reason, which faculty have a voice in the selection of a chair and which do not (as noted in chapter 3) is an important consideration. Although predicting how a particular individual will perform is impossible, participants noted a number of considerations that relate to departmental collegiality for NTTF.

Henry, a NTTF at RU, noted that how chairs think about hiring and what counts as expertise (e.g., experience teaching versus experience researching) can shape a department in both membership and attitude toward fixed-term faculty. Nicole (chair, MU) contrasted a prior administrator who she described as "amazing" with a new hire who came from outside the institution. The incoming person came from a research intensive university that was not collectively bargained and struggled to understand and adapt to the important differences in those environments. Quite likely, this person was hired in part *because* of representing institutional aspiration, but the lack of organizational awareness and acclimation negatively affected collegiality.

Ultimately, as Nicole (chair, MU) emphasized and the preceding chapters suggested, chairs can do a lot to redirect how NTTF are thought of and included through political, symbolic, and interpersonal approaches. Culture change is possible over time, and the seemingly small decisions highlighted in the previous chapters that recognize expertise and operate with interpersonal trust and respect in meetings, communications, interpersonal interactions, and resource use are noticed by the members of a department. In departments where collegiality is already thriving, for chairs to anticipate inevitable changes in environment, membership, policy, curriculum, and other factors supports an agile and healthy collegiality.

## Spatial, Material, and Financial Resources

Although departments are organizational phenomena, how they function and how they are experienced are strongly influenced by physical and financial realities. Departments are necessarily place-based and shaped, over time, by the quality and quantity of spaces available for offices, labs, classrooms, meeting rooms, and common gathering areas (Gieryn, 2002). Spaces are important in and of themselves, and the relative position of those spaces in relation to the geographic campus contributes to perceptions of belonging and identity. Additionally, material resources (e.g., copiers, computers, lab equipment) and financial resources (e.g., money for professional development, summer teaching) and the basis on which these resources are allocated are important factors in a department's collegial environment, conveying symbolic messages of equitability or hierarchy. All of these considerations coalesce into one of two categories frequently raised in our interviews: the importance of contexts and resources and the use and distribution of resources within a department.

*Contexts and Resources*

The constraining realities of physical space on campus are a challenge to most departments. There is seldom sufficient space (e.g., not enough offices) or seldom sufficient match of space types or amounts and departmental needs (e.g., conference room is too small). Even when faculty members have the opportunity to participate in the design of departmental spaces, they struggle to anticipate how to allot space to effectively meet the variety of needs (Alleman, Holly, & Costello, 2013). However obvious these points are as generalizations, the particularities of a department's space can significantly shape factors such as the quality, quantity, and nature of interactions among colleagues; the operation of organizational processes (e.g., meeting participation); and the development of subgroup cultures (e.g., clumping of faculty by employment type), which in turn shape departmental collegiality for NTTF. For example, several faculty from a department at MU described a split of offices between two hallways, one with a reputation as the "fun" hall and the other as the "quiet" hall. This physical division, participants noted, had the potential to exacerbate differences of professional roles that are the basis of office assignments if stereotypes and hall loyalty replaced meaningful interaction.

The effects of space and resource limitations should not be presumed to be linear: Outcomes are more complicated than a one-to-one relationship between adequate space and collegial climate. One department at RU was split between two parts of an older, remodeled building, but faculty of various ranks and statuses insisted that the effect was not isolating or bifurcating. Rather, as both office areas had clusters of faculty across employment types, common spaces (a conference room and a break room) drew colleagues together. In one department at MU, the dearth of office spaces and intermingling with offices from other departments made the sense of group identity more challenging to establish, even while required office sharing may promote dyadic relationships.

At both institutions, participants noted how common spaces such as the mailbox area or the work room can facilitate group interaction that would not otherwise happen. Sabrina, a TTF in STEM Department at MU, saw the potential for her department's modest space to further facilitate communication and interaction:

> We only have a quote, unquote "common room" that is, you know, it serves as a mail room and there is a little table in there but it's not really a coffee area. There is a coffee machine, but we don't have a really good meeting space that would invite people to sit down and have a coffee, even just for

five minutes. It's more like you standing in the mail room and you happen walk across somebody's path who's just coming to get coffee and then you chat for three sentences. That is a good starting point, but I believe to improve that environment further that part would be a very easy thing to bring to a new level by adding a couch, by throwing out some boxes that nobody wants to look at to create space.

Sabrina's assessment included a notation of spatial limitation (i.e., "we don't really have a good meeting space") as well a recommendation for improved use, a segue to our second point of emphasis: the use of resources.

## Use and Distribution of Resources Within a Department

Obviously, many spatial realities, such as offices on multiple floors, are beyond the control of a department. In cases like this, department members must make efforts to offset the liabilities of space constraints, such as promoting interactions via scheduling regular lunches to bridge office distribution divisions. However, in other cases chairs and department members need to consider what modifications or repurposing efforts are possible that might better leverage available spatial, material, and financial resources, as Sabrina's ideas for renovating the mailroom imply.

In some situations, the benefits or liabilities of spatial constraints are equitably shared, such as inadequate common spaces or classrooms. In others, constraints seem to disproportionately affect NTTF, such as office assignment preferences or distribution of professional development funds based on rank rather than seniority or professional need. For instance, a NTTF at MU was pushed out of a desirable office because a tenured faculty member wanted it. By contrast, Michael (NTTF, MU) described an effort to equitably distribute access to coveted offices with windows:

> We allocate offices somewhat based on seniority, but seniority is not about tenured or lecturer. It's about how long they've been with us. We have a faculty member who's been here 35 years. He got dibs on a window. That only seemed fair. Then the 2 faculty members who have been here for 20 years got windows. We have 2 lecturers in offices with windows, because they've been here 10 years.

Participants also noted a third category of effect that occurs when departments face limited or insufficient resources: Faculty who may already feel marginalized (e.g., NTTF, women, faculty of color) might interpret a department's lack of provision for them or lack of readiness to provide material resources, such as an up-to-date computer, as a reflection of their "less-than" status. Daniel, an administrator at MU who began his career as a NTTF, commented on this as a lost opportunity to draw in new faculty that can end up producing the opposite result:

> Well, it's very easy to feel devalued. We are not paid a whole lot. When you walk into a place and nobody knows your name and your office is not very nice and you have trouble logging on to be able to get your access. Here you are showing up early because you want to be responsible and you're excited about joining this [unit], and then, the university is not ready for you. That's a terrible message to send to folks.

When faculty from historically marginalized groups perceive that their needs for computers, work space, or other resources have not been attended to, their sense of second-class status is likely to increase. Even if, in some cases, the source of the problem is a paucity of departmental resources that cuts across all members of the department, lack of access to resources might well be interpreted as a slight against those on the margins because they are not privy to the logic of distribution. In such cases, creating spatial and resource logics that are consistent, transparent, and equitable, such as Michael's example of office distribution, conveys to all members that they are valued despite less than optimal resource access.

## The Context Model of Collegiality

With the five elements now more fully explored, understanding the nature of their relationship with one another becomes paramount. In Figure 4.1 we identify the five context factors described in this chapter and place them in dynamic relationship with one another and with departmental collegiality. The lesson is that no one of these factors functions in isolation. For example, departmental spatial, material, and financial resources, as a category, can be a challenging element of departmental history when needs have not been met in the past. Yes, we know that at first glance the model looks complicated, with lots of lines. However, we encourage you not to overthink the variety of connections—they link every point to every other point, highlighting the complexity of inter-relationships. Considering the nature of the connections between and among various of the five factors can be an instructive exercise.

## Conclusion

This chapter highlighted the range of contextual factors beyond current departmental membership, policies, and behaviors that are likely to shape

**Figure 4.1.** The context model of collegiality.

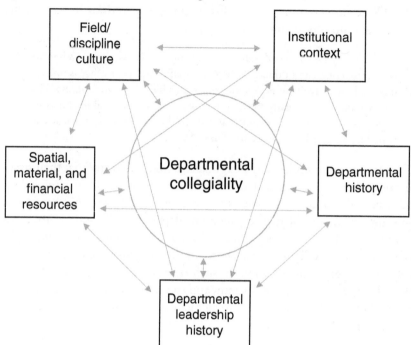

the nature and task of departmental collegiality, particularly for NTTF, in a given context. Although much of what we have discussed can be thought of in terms of constraints over which little direct control can be exercised—field/disciplinary cultures, institutional context, departmental and chair histories, and spatial/resource realities—the examples throughout this chapter highlight ways in which each of these categories also represents opportunities for new imagination and agency. Where field/disciplinary cultures isolate, where institutional expectations prioritize research over teaching, where departmental history offers little but the pain of exclusion, and where offices separate faculty, opportunities yet abound. Leadership can provide equitable and clear space use policies, colleagues can commit to deliberate and regular departmental rituals (e.g., lunches, research talks, celebrations of accomplishments), and collaborative scholarly and service projects that recognize the contributions of all members can enrich the soil where the growth of collegiality can occur over generations.

As the two vignettes at the opening of this chapter illustrate, departmental context is a confluence of opportunities and difficulties, some the result of circumstance, and some the result of leadership, behaviors, or policies of the past. The faculty in the two case departments, notable for the quality of collegiality for NTTF, were clear about both the tenuousness of collegiality and the factors that continue to support it, such as vocal support from the chair, valuing contributions of all kinds, and deliberately hiring for collegiality. The focus on context here highlights the importance of leveraging situational resources (e.g., good common spaces, a history of respecting NTTF as professionals) and from them distilling shared values (e.g., "we respect the contributions of all faculty members") to become priorities deliberately pursued, in order to build sustainable collegial cultures for NTTF and all faculty.

## Recommendations for Leveraging Institutional Context

As Hardy (1991) cautioned, collegiality is not a natural state of affairs, one that can be assumed. Rather collegiality must be nurtured and tended on an ongoing basis. A host of factors can either aid or constrain collegiality. Limited resources might create competition among faculty, resulting in friction that impairs collegiality. Shared space might bring people together to interact and build positive relationships—or lead faculty to create schedules where they seldom see each other. In short, as we noted at the start of this chapter, context matters. Moreover, not all of the context factors are within institutional control (e.g., limited external funding, disciplinary culture). Here, we outline five recommendations for how administrators, department chairs, and faculty can attend to institutional context in ways that promote collegiality.

1. Take the long view: With so many tasks and challenges competing for individuals' time, it can be easy to lose sight of the need to tend to a collegiality culture. However, collegiality untended can wither on the vine. It is important that practices, processes, and decisions be undertaken through the lens of collegiality. Do the decisions made reflect the shared purpose of the department or institution? Were faculty, including NTTF, consulted and included in the decision-making process? Do processes reflect a presumption of inclusion and transparency?

2. Invest in department chairs: Department chairs are central in the long-term aspect of tending to collegiality, and some level of continuity in approach between chairs in a department is important to building and maintaining collegial spaces. Thus, institutions must invest in the department chair role. One way to do this is to hire wise, which includes identifying faculty who are likely to be strong department chairs early in their careers and develop them along the way. Once in

their positions, chairs need regular professional development that not only builds essential skills (e.g., management, faculty development) but also supports acting with a collegial mind-set.

3. Hire for collegiality: As noted in this chapter, the expectations and outlooks of individual faculty can make an enormous difference in shaping the collegial climate. This suggests departments should be hiring faculty with their dispositions to collegiality in mind. Assessing this can be admittedly difficult, but interview topics such as how the candidate handles conflict, checking references in this regard, and the like can give a sense for how well a potential hire would contribute to or interfere with a collegial culture.

4. Attend to the "small" stuff: Much of how faculty experience institutional context is through seemingly little things. How office space is allocated, whether one's new office is cleaned and ready for arrival, constantly shifting mailboxes, and other considerations are symbols of (lack of) respect and permanence. Administrators and department chairs must be mindful of the potentially large impact of these small things in shaping collegial spaces for NTTF.

5. Assess collegial culture: For departmental members and leaders seeking to diagnose and nurture their own collegiality climate, we recommend using the context model of collegiality (Figure 4.1) to perform a collegiality context scan. You can do so through the following process:

   a. Write down a few words that describe the current state of departmental collegiality (central circle).

   b. List the ways that the global sense of departmental collegiality, particularly for NTTF, has changed, developed, or shifted over the course of each member's career.

   c. Look at the five contextual factors, and invite faculty members to list specifics of their department that pertain to each factor.

   d. Label the arrows that connect the five factors to one another with specific descriptions of how the particular features of each factor listed in step c interact to shape collegiality.

   e. Highlight those points of intersection that seem to naturally promote collegiality and those that seem to impede it.

   f. Discuss how the strengths and resources of the department might be harnessed to address or redefine the areas of challenge to collegiality.

# 5

## CONCLUSION

*No one's work life is made more tolerable and productive when a person feels excluded from the social ties that others have.—Stewart and Valian (2018), p. 270*

*The higher education community must rethink the academic career, the organization of faculty work, and how to make best use of and support all faculty members in their varied roles. To do this, we must revisit the historic relationships between faculty members and their institutions.—Gappa, Austin, and Trice (2005), p. 36*

*There's a place for everybody in an academic department. . . . [NTTF] too are members of the community. Recognizing their role in a nonhierarchical fashion is what I think really collegiality is.—Dana, Administrator, MU*

Higher education is in a time of significant change and challenge. Accountability pressures such as performance-based funding are pushing public institutions to rethink curricula and instruction and stretching resources. Colleges and universities continue to seek ways to effectively serve an increasingly diverse student population, as well as respond to growing public concern about student debt and the steep cost of higher education. These challenges, even if not all negative, can spark feelings of insecurity and even anxiety among faculty and staff and in turn strain professional behavior and relationships (Cipriano, 2011). Strains in these relationships make it all the more difficult for institutions to respond to the challenges in proactive and thoughtful ways that maintain their health and the ability to accomplish their missions.

At times such as these, the collegial ideal may be one of our most important resources. The behaviors and values associated with collegiality grease the wheels of academic governance, allowing for an open exchange of ideas and information in pursuit of shared goals in a climate of trust and respect. Collegiality also has less tangible benefits, such as contributing to a work environment that faculty value (Boice, 1992; Rice, Sorcinelli, & Austin 2000; Tierney & Bensimon, 1996), shaping commitment to the institution (Barnes, Agago, & Coombs, 1998), and enhancing professional satisfaction (Bode, 1999). The benefits of collegiality may be especially critical now in helping colleges and universities respond to the changing landscape of higher education.

Yet, ironically, these very forces of change simultaneously make collegiality even more difficult to access and the collegial ideal more difficult to attain. The emergence of the NTTF role late in the twentieth century was itself a result of some of the forces of change just described (e.g., rising costs, the need for flexibility in faculty staffing and structures). NTTF were employed as a solution to these changes, but the formation of the NTTF role was perceived as a threat to the TTF role (Kezar & Sam, 2010b). As a result, NTTF have typically existed at the margins of the collegium, with highly inconsistent, conditional access to the rights and responsibilities associated with collegiality that TTF often take for granted (Haviland et al., 2017; Waltman et al., 2012). Only recently have scholars begun to raise questions about where NTTF might fit in this collegial ideal (Alleman & Haviland, 2016; Haviland et al., 2017; Kezar & Sam, 2010b; Ott & Cisneros, 2015). The growing sense that NTTF are partners and colleagues rather than a problematic academic population in need of management (Kezar & Sam, 2010b) is a promising shift in perspective, and in our work we have sought to learn from those departments that have successfully supported and engaged NTTF as colleagues.

We have shared the stories, examples, and practices that come from departments that are healthy, positive collegial spaces for NTTF. In our research for this book, we were heartened to hear examples of collegiality for all faculty. Faculty spoke enthusiastically about the virtues of collegiality and described ways they sought to nurture and grow this important resource. Even as they were clear about the challenges, and the need to continually tend the collegial garden, they were equally clear about the benefits and the importance of doing so.

As we said at the start of this book, some (by no means all) of the lessons and strategies contained here are very simple and perhaps even obvious. This fact might be discouraging, leading one to wonder why departments and institutions are not doing these things with NTTF already. However, we are optimistic because we see departments and institutions struggling with these questions to create a positive collegial climate for NTTF and all faculty. Rather than searching for a single silver bullet, they recognize that collegiality for NTTF in particular, as the quote by Gappa et al. (2005) at the start of this chapter suggests, involves taking new perspectives on faculty work and expertise relative to the tenure-normative model. These departments and institutions are aware of new faculty roles, exploring how these varied roles contribute to institutional mission, and striving to find ways to shape behavior, culture, and structure (Bess, 1992) in ways that recognize NTTF as colleagues.

In this final chapter, we pull together the lessons learned from these healthy departments related to shaping collegial environments for NTTF. We focus on what we have learned from our research for how TTF, department chairs, and administrators can support collegiality for NTTF. We begin with a brief overview of the major ideas covered in chapters 2 through 4 before articulating several "big ideas" that our research suggests are important for shaping collegiality for NTTF.

## Conclusions

At its core, collegiality for all faculty, including NTTF, is nurtured by attending to the personal, the professional, and the contextual. Collegiality is driven by a combination of trust and respect for the faculty member—both as a person and as a professional—fostered within a larger ecosystem reflecting structural factors, institutional cultures, disciplinary characteristics, and departmental history. There are surely tensions for departments and their faculty in working through these dimensions; even the healthy departments we studied were challenged at times to navigate personality differences, policy limitations, a history of exclusive practices, or faculty subgroups who were not necessarily "on board" with recognizing NTTF as colleagues. In addition, as we described, gender, race, and ethnicity shaped collegial experiences, and not always in positive ways. However, on balance, the departments were able to build positive collegial spaces by cultivating interpersonal trust and respect, recognizing professional expertise, and understanding the role of context.

### *Interpersonal Trust and Respect*

The presence of interpersonal trust and respect (the personal dimension), discussed in chapter 2, was a cornerstone of collegiality in general and for NTTF in particular. This sense of trust and respect emerged through an iterative cycle, where faculty members interacted with and got to know one another as not only professors but also people. These interactions fostered a sense of trust and regard for one another. Collegiality for NTTF was shaped by a recognition that all faculty, regardless of rank, status, or credentials, shared a common humanity and were working fundamentally toward the same goal (e.g., student learning), which transcended the status distinctions and hierarchies typical of faculty life.

Tierney (2008) has noted that a sense of respect and appreciation foundational to interpersonal trust are built through personal relationships. Based on our data, these relationships can emerge from a range of interactions. For some, as Bess (1992) suggests, these interactions might be more organic and grow from an individual's "personal need" (p. 24)—a desire to connect with and get to know others. A hallway hello might turn into an extended conversation about a child's soccer team, a recent sporting event, or a problem in one's class. Other interactions might be facilitated by and take place at department events (business or social). A chat before a department meeting might turn into coffee or lunch to finish the conversation.

In the healthy departments, these interactions helped participants acknowledge personal as well as professional commonalities. Participants saw that all faculty, including NTTF, had professional goals and aspirations, good days and bad, and personal/family demands outside of the university. Appreciating that faculty shared basic human qualities and experiences then prompted additional availability, invitations, and efforts to include NTTF in activities and events. Stewart and Valian (2018), quoted at the start of this chapter, refer to this appreciation of the human needs of faculty members by acknowledging that who we are as people affects who we are and how we act as professionals.

The interactions and relationships between and among faculty also shaped a trust and personal respect that facilitated the work of the department. Did differences, misunderstandings, and other basic challenges of human interaction arise? Of course! And issues of race, ethnicity, and gender created strains, such as the incorrect assumption by colleagues that Carrie's (NTTF, RU) research agenda focused on people of color. However, the personal relationships and knowledge of one another that had been cultivated helped faculty members navigate interpersonal difficulties by recognizing a sense of shared purpose even at times of disagreement.

In healthy departments, even if faculty disagreed on how to get there, they presumed that each individual ultimately had the same end in mind and was acting in good faith to achieve that shared goal rather than, perhaps, undermine a colleague. To be sure, making the choice to suspend mistrust at a time of conflict or believe that a colleague was acting toward the same goal rather than trying to advance self-interests involved a personal choice to accept some level of risk and believe others were acting in good faith. However, the interpersonal trust and respect that had been built meant the perceived level of risk was much lower. Thus, as Greg A. (Administrator, RU) explained, faculty might say a prayer to begin their meeting, disagree heartily with each other in the meeting, and then head off to a group lunch afterward.

### *Recognition of Professional Expertise*

Complementing the personal component of trust and respect is the recognition of professional expertise, the condition or ticket for admission to the collegium, addressed in chapter 3. Arguably, at least for TTF, the process for earning this recognition is relatively clear and consistent, with expertise defined by agreed-on criteria and assessed over time relative to these criteria. TTF demonstrate expertise first (typically) through advanced study and then subsequent experience as professors, ultimately earning tenure and promotion.

Policies, procedures, and common practices exist to guide this certification process, with time lines for earning tenure and promotion generally standard across the profession. As they move up the professorial ladder and demonstrate expertise as recognized by their peers, TTF earn professional trust and respect and are seen as experts. Moreover, as noted in chapter 1, institutions also have rational reasons for why TTF at different levels can or cannot participate in specific governance activities. Ultimately, the general clarity of policies, processes, and practices (e.g., for tenure and promotion, for participation in governance, and even broader concepts such as academic freedom) related to TTF demonstrates a sense of institutional trust in and respect for the expertise of professors.

At many institutions, NTTF lack the opportunity to be recognized for their professional expertise. With their work heavily focused on teaching and service, NTTF are typically excluded from or have little time for the professional activity through which expertise is typically demonstrated and recognized: scholarship. In addition, with opportunities for NTTF to advance along a career path similar to TTF ranks typically limited or nonexistent, they lack the opportunity for peer review and certification that is such a central component to the recognition of expertise for TTF and entrance into the collegium. The consideration, then, is how institutions and academia more generally can find ways to recognize the expertise that NTTF contribute on a daily basis.

The healthy collegial departments we studied found ways to challenge, or at least work around, the tenure-normative model to recognize the expertise of their NTTF colleagues and disrupt a faculty hierarchy driven by tenure and scholarship. These departments and their faculty recognized and valued the contributions of NTTF in terms of teaching and service (e.g., program leadership, committee participation) as furthering the department's mission and demonstrating NTTF expertise, not merely freeing up TTF to do the "more important" work of scholarship. Such recognition was both formal (e.g., awards, voting rights) and informal (e.g., kind words, seeking NTTF input).

These departments and, sometimes, their universities, also recognized and nurtured NTTF expertise in other ways. First, they invested in their NTTF colleagues by doing their best to craft work assignments that reflected the NTTF interests, evaluated them based on their job descriptions (not tenure-normative expectations), and facilitated professional growth and development. Second, and perhaps most notably, they engaged NTTF in decision-making (e.g., committee work, voting, department meetings) and sought their input. They did so not just to relieve TTF of service burdens, but because they knew that NTTF had expertise that was important to the department.

Of course, these efforts were not always easy, and they did not always create the ideal recognition of NTTF expertise. In many cases, particularly when such recognition and inclusion happened at the department level, recognition happened via informal workarounds enacted at the discretion of the chair or TTF or both. For example, we know, anecdotally, of one department (not part of this study) that chose to disregard stated university rules about NTTF voting rights to better enfranchise NTTF. Although we learned in the first phase of our research that these workarounds were often appreciated by NTTF, at other times the very need for a workaround reinforced NTTF perceptions of being marginalized (Haviland et al., 2017). This point highlights the tension that can exist between department values around collegiality and the institutional policies that may not reflect those values. It also highlights the need to think about how to be intentional about recognizing and drawing on NTTF expertise across departmental, institutional, and professional levels (Bess, 1992; Haviland et al., 2017), so that larger structures align with more local values and culture.

## The Role of Context

The positive collegial relationships in the departments we studied took place within layers of context that shaped, spurred on, and sometimes abated the personal and professional regard underlying collegiality. As we have noted, addressing and shaping context is a long-term endeavor; context can wax and wane over time as personnel changes, resources ebb and flow, and leadership comes and goes. Returning to the metaphor from chapter 1—collegiality is not in fact a given, but rather a condition that must be fed, watered, and nurtured in ways that reflect local conditions; it is, and must be, organic.

The context or culture of these healthy departments honored and sought to facilitate that imperative in a variety of ways. The departments were mindful of the institutions' identities and missions, using these as frameworks to understand their colleagues and appreciate the contributions of NTTF. At RU, the Christian identity was central to not only attracting faculty but also understanding, as Andrew (NTTF) said, that "all of us are works in progress" and therefore deserving of patience and understanding. At MU, the focus on serving first-generation and low-income students informed a general solidarity in the work of all faculty and the value of NTTF contributions.

The departments were also mindful of both the presence of NTTF in their immediate community and how the broader context might influence NTTF experiences. For instance, at least one department (Humanities, RU) explicitly asked faculty in the department to think about the NTTF role and how the department could continue to integrate NTTF as colleagues even as institutional focus on scholarship grew. At MU, the chair of Social Science Department met with NTTF as a group on a regular basis, recognizing they might have interests, perspectives, and questions distinct from TTF. These meetings signaled a culture seeking to address NTTF needs. Chairs and faculty in general were also mindful of broader factors (e.g., office locations, mailboxes, even commutes) and structured activities such as social events and department meetings in ways that allowed for maximum participation of all faculty, including NTTF. They shaped spaces, literal and figurative, for faculty to get to know each other personally and professionally, to develop a sense of shared mission and team. In these departments an ethos of transparency, with information shared freely and with all, and broad participation in decision-making was present.

Central to tending this culture are the department chair and senior faculty (both tenured and NTTF) who set the tone, model behavior, and play significant roles in setting both policy and informal practice that reflect and shape departmental culture. Collegiality for NTTF in the healthy departments benefitted from an ongoing effort, particularly by chairs, to include, recognize, and support NTTF as colleagues. It was often the chair who sought NTTF input, encouraged professional development, and drove the recognition of NTTF expertise. Building a culture of collegiality for NTTF and all faculty took time, a shared commitment, and ongoing effort. To the extent departments were able to build such a culture, a continuum of chairs was needed to do so.

As we conclude this section, we return to the figure we introduced in chapter 1, shown here as Figure 5.1. This figure provided a visual for how we see the role of the personal, the professional, and context in shaping collegial spaces for all faculty, including NTTF.

**Figure 5.1.** Elements contributing to collegial experiences for faculty.

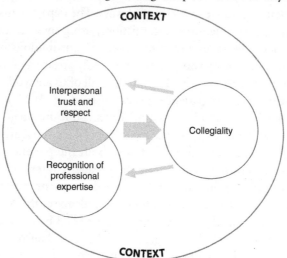

In this book, we have separated the personal (interpersonal trust and respect) and the professional (expertise) for our purposes. However, as should be evident by now, these are not discrete components of positive collegial environments for NTTF and others. Rather, the personal and professional interact in symbiotic ways. The social lunch is a time for faculty to talk more honestly about departmental politics and problems. Shared committee service builds a familiarity that leads faculty to pitch in for one another to cover classes or professional obligations during a time of family need or personal crisis. The relationship built through repeated hallway conversations and more extended interactions encourages collaboration and consultation between NTTF and TTF for syllabus development or an instructional challenge—a recognition of professional expertise built initially through casual interaction.

Separating the personal and professional is a forced distinction, at least as it relates to shaping collegial spaces for NTTF. The challenge for departments, institutions, and the profession is to find ways to integrate both the personal and professional dimensions of faculty work lives in ways that support a culture of inclusion and collegiality for NTTF. In the next section, we offer core principles we believe are important for creating this culture.

## Principles for an Inclusive Collegium

We have noted that the collegium is organic; it is up to faculty to shape and nurture the collegium they want. The collegium of today, the one grown and shaped during an era when tenure was the norm and scholarship the paramount marker of expertise, must be reconceptualized if we are to meet the needs of students, faculty, and institutions in today's era of differentiated faculty roles. The new collegium must be one that is far more inclusive than what currently exists. If the idea of the collegium seems like a quaint notion from the twelfth century, then the *inclusive collegium* is far more radical, calling on us to rethink the exclusive nature of the collegium, attend to personal and professional relationships, reconsider how we go about recognizing experience, and speak openly and with intention about what collegiality means.

In this section, we offer a handful of principles we see as central to building this more inclusive collegium for NTTF. The responsibility for shaping and nurturing this ethos of inclusion rests squarely on the shoulders of TTF, department chairs, and campus administrators. In today's higher education, it is these individuals who make and interpret the rules and engage in the informal practices that shape departmental and institutional culture.

In making this point, we do not mean to perpetuate what we see as an unhealthy power imbalance. Indeed, we see a role for NTTF who are more established and secure in their positions and have access to formal levers of power as partners in shaping more collegial spaces for NTTF. However, NTTF in general are well aware of the hierarchy that shapes faculty life, as well as their place in that hierarchy. Seldom will they dare to assume that they are included in the interpersonal and professional life of the department, particularly if they are relatively new and/or in less secure positions. Therefore, at this moment in time, it is up to TTF, chairs, and administrators to be explicit about inviting NTTF into the collegium in small and more significant ways.

In the remaining pages, we offer several principles for how to create this culture of inclusive collegiality and counteract the exclusive hierarchy that typically excludes NTTF.

### *Presume Inclusion*

Our first principle calls on faculty and administrators to apply the same inclusive lens to NTTF that is applied to TTF, rather than seeing the former as an "other" that enjoys only conditional access to collegiality. As we noted in chapter 1, involvement of TTF in the work life of the department (e.g., department meetings, committee service) is presumed, with exclusion needing to be justified (e.g., potential conflict of interest, faculty rank relative to the work of the committee). With rare exceptions, TTF can choose whether to participate or not; in the most collegial of spaces, they can assume that their rights and interests will be honored even when they are not present. In contrast, NTTF have inconsistent and varied access to attending meetings and serving on committees, limited and conditional voting rights, and uneven access to professional development and career advancement (Haviland et al., 2017).

When we saw collegiality work for NTTF, we witnessed a premise that they could participate in the life of the department in more or less the same ways as their TTF colleagues, and, indeed, that their participation was indeed desired and valued. Although the NTTF might choose to not attend a meeting, or skip a lunch, or miss a social event, the choice was theirs to make. They knew they could join a hallway conversation if they wished, serve on a range of committees that matched their expertise, and contribute to the future of the department. They knew they were respected because they were included in the interpersonal and professional life of the department.

## Expand Conceptions of Expertise Beyond Traditional Notions of Scholarship and Expertise

Our second principle challenges institutions and the faculty profession to expand traditional definitions of *scholarship* and *expertise*. Boyer (1990), Rice (1986), and others pushed for an expanded view of scholarship and expertise at a time when the NTTF role was just emerging and being solidified in higher education. While they presumably did not write with NTTF in mind, they were prescient in recognizing that scholarship (and with it, expertise) was far broader than empirical research. Their call is as relevant and important to consider today as the structure of the faculty evolves and access to collegiality is further strained.

Our work suggests the faculty profession must rethink how we conceptualize and recognize the expertise that is the condition for admission into the collegium. If NTTF are to be included as colleagues, as partners rather than second-class workers, higher education must find ways to disrupt the tenure-normative model and, with it, the nearly exclusive link between empirical scholarship and expertise. The current model virtually ensures that NTTF will remain on the margins of the collegium, admitted in small ways only when it suits TTF needs. The healthy departments in this study found formal (e.g., having NTTF teach upper division and graduate course) and informal (e.g., seeking input, awards and recognition) ways to transcend this model, honor the expertise NTTF brought, and incorporate it to the benefit of their department.

## Attend to Personal and Professional Relationships

Our third principle speaks to the need for institutions and departments to be intentional about facilitating the development of personal and professional relationships between and among faculty. Although faculty work may appear solitary and even isolating to some, much of faculty work is social; beyond hallway conversations, faculty interact around academic governance and collaborate on teaching and research, for instance. In the healthy departments we studied, the interactions, knowing, and relationships that developed among faculty contributed to and grew from both personal and professional respect that was foundational to collegiality for NTTF. These relationships allowed NTTF and TTF to know one another as people, develop appreciation for each other's expertise, and establish a sense of trust and team.

To be sure, many of these relationships are organic, developing as faculty go about their daily business. Yet these relationships also blossom when faculty come to know each other at semester- or year-end celebrations, work together on projects, meet for lunch or coffee between classes, or learn more about one another's work and accomplishments in department meetings. In our experience, a good portion of personal knowing takes place as faculty engage in their service work in the department or institution. Thus, to the degree NTTF are excluded from these spaces, they are also likely excluded from the opportunity to develop these relationships and earn personal and professional respect from their colleagues—a point that has relevance to our next principle. Departments and institutions must attend to creating spaces and opportunities for faculty to interact and build the relationships foundational to collegiality.

### *Attend to Policies and Practices*

Our fourth principle highlights the need to attend to policies and practices in ways that facilitate the inclusion of NTTF in the life and work of the department and the institution. This principle has at least two dimensions. First, policies and practices must be shaped with the premise of inclusion, with exclusion needing to be justified, just as is the case for TTF. In terms of service, why should NTTF not serve on curriculum committees? In terms of voting, should NTTF be allowed to vote for department chair? We think so. Should they have a vote in recommendations for hiring other NTTF? We believe, yes. What about recommendations for hiring TTF? If we are serious about breaking down the hierarchy, then why not? Ultimately, the question should be "why not" rather than "why" as it relates to NTTF inclusion in governance, just as it is for TTF. If NTTF are not actively engaged in decision-making (through department meetings, service, and voting), then they merely work for rather than with TTF, tasked with carrying out work others delegate to them. Our shared goal must be to determine consistent and well-thought-out criteria for NTTF participation, just as we have for TTF, grounded in and reflective of broadened conceptualizations of expertise.

Second, clarity, consistency, and alignment of policies across campus is imperative if NTTF are going to truly be included as colleagues. Departmental autonomy worked to the benefit of collegiality for NTTF in the healthy departments we studied, as the departments shaped policies and practices for inclusion; as noted previously, we even know of one department that ignored institutional policies that disenfranchised NTTF. However, less healthy departments marginalized NTTF in the absence of clear institutional policy. Moreover, NTTF across MU and RU were well aware of the departments where NTTF had more or fewer rights, thus establishing their positive experiences as a privilege for which they should be grateful rather than a norm which any NTTF should have the right to expect.

Attending to structure via policies and practices is a necessary but not sufficient measure to ensure collegiality for NTTF. Given the significant interpersonal dimension of collegiality in terms of trust and respect, inclusive policies and practices can only do so much to achieve collegiality for NTTF. Indeed, as Bess (1992) has noted, the fact that culture generally trumps structure is what prompts department chairs and faculty to implement workarounds to limiting or unclear institutional structures and allows the healthy departments to exist. However, culture alone cannot sustain collegiality. Clear and consistent policies and practices can provide for a more robust and sustainable collegiality for NTTF. Based on our work, more leadership in this area is needed at the institutional level in particular to promote clarity, consistency, and accountability.

## Nurture and Model Collegiality

Our fifth principle points to the need to be explicit and transparent about what collegiality means and why it is important. As we noted at the start of this book, *collegiality* is a commonly used but not well-understood term. As a concept central to faculty life and academic governance, it deserves far more time, attention, and intentionality than it is typically given. Moreover, a sense of collegiality and belonging can be very easy to undermine, particularly for NTTF. Recently, on one of our campuses, an administrator sent out an e-mail to all faculty noting that "faculty and lecturers" were eligible for an opportunity. The e-mail was met quickly with a correction from a NTTF: Lecturers are faculty, although the phrasing suggested otherwise. It was a small but significant slip that cast a shadow on an otherwise inclusive act.

As an academic community we must tend to and jealously guard the collegial ideal. This means being clear about what it means and not taking it for granted. Faculty, department chairs, and administrators must talk regularly and explicitly about collegiality—what it means, what it does and does not look like in practice, whether policies demonstrate collegiality, civility, and respect, as well as who (including NTTF, as well as members of minoritized groups) has access to it and under what conditions. Actions that undermine collegiality are typically microaggressive, happening in little ways that progressively nick the collegial culture over time. Being able to recognize and name these transgressions is the first step in addressing them, which is why honest conversations about collegiality are so important.

This imperative includes being mindful of the connection between collegiality and an increasingly diverse faculty. Being a "good colleague" means that all faculty, but particularly those with positions of privilege and power, honor and advocate for the interests of their faculty colleagues regardless of social identity. Given that much of the growing diversity among the faculty is reflected in the NTTF group, while TTF are still predominantly White and male, conversations around collegiality and NTTF must make this standard transparent. It should not just be a TTF from the same minoritized social group (e.g., Latinx, female) who advocates for a NTTF with a shared identity. Similarly, specific service obligations should not fall disproportionately on some groups more than others, and department chairs and TTF must be alert to these imbalances. Good colleagues, particularly those with the greatest privilege, are mindful of and seek to remedy such inequities. Collegiality means honoring diverse colleagues and diverse perspectives.

These conversations are all the more important because collegiality is a complicated concept that can be misunderstood and, worse, misused. The idea of collegiality can be used to stifle constructive dissent and debate, in direct contrast to its call for open, rational dialogue.

Silencing a less popular view about pedagogical style for the sake of appeasing the greater good, for instance, likely silences the voice of a marginalized faculty member and, quite possibly, the marginalized students being represented. And collegiality can be used as a tool to exclude scholars who do not fit the normative model of faculty: White, male, and heterosexual. Indeed, as we have described, the homogeneity of the faculty even today leads some faculty (e.g., Leah, Maya) to self-silence and monitor contributions. Good collegiality seeks to prevent this climate.

The concept of *fit*, for instance, has been used as a code (perhaps unconsciously) to decide that a faculty candidate from a minoritized group should be the second rather than first choice in a search so as not to disrupt the cohesiveness of a faculty body. Similarly, someone might be labeled a "bad colleague" for rightly challenging taken-for-granted norms or practices. *Collegiality* does not mean uniformity, agreement, and consistency—although some may see these as the goal. The risk of collegiality being misunderstood or misused makes conversations about what collegiality is and is not critical.

Related, modeling collegiality and holding others accountable for uncollegial behaviors is important for everyone from administrators to faculty. In one of our healthy departments, the chair recounted having to confront and redirect a TTF who had marginalized a NTTF in the department. The conversation did not go well, but a line was drawn. Similarly, senior faculty (TTF or NTTF) might be in a position to challenge the exclusion of NTTF from decision-making spaces or identify instances where NTTF might feel compelled to "volunteer" for additional work given their tenuous status.

However, holding others accountable in this way means not only recognizing the behaviors (in this case, the transgression was glaring) but also having and using the skills and language to frame the issue and engage the problem. Thus, institutions must ensure that their chairs, deans, and mid-level administrators in particular, but also faculty, are prepared for driving these difficult, conflict-laden conversations (Cipriano, 2011), as well as have the ability to frame these conversations in the context of collegiality and institutional values.

## Final Words

As we hope is clear at this stage, we believe collegiality in general, and for NTTF in particular, is essential to the health of higher education. Simply put, collegiality matters. When it works, collegiality makes our institutions better by allowing faculty to engage in shared problem-solving; it also makes faculty work more positive and satisfying. However, conceptions of collegiality, and in particular who gets access to it and how, have not kept pace with the changing structure of the faculty. As a result, NTTF are often left on the outside looking in, despite having the same credentials and doing work that looks very similar to that of TTF.

No one is well served when a sizeable portion of the full-time faculty is left on the outside of the collegium with no clear path for admission. NTTF themselves feel marginalized, disrespected, and unappreciated. TTF, declining as a percentage of full-time faculty overall, face increasing service burdens; NTTF, increasing in numbers, have limited opportunities for participation in service. Ultimately, students suffer when NTTF, who do a substantial portion of the instruction on many campuses, are disconnected from or unaware of departmental initiatives and programs for students and unable to shape curricula. And everyone (institutions, faculty, and students) suffers when much of the diversity higher education claims to seek grows in the NTTF ranks, and those individuals are then excluded from spaces where they might be able to shape policies, practices, and curricula that support all students.

This current state does not have to remain. The healthy departments we studied remind us that the collegium is organic, shaped and defined by its members (Bennett, 1998). These healthy departments have responded to the changing faculty structure by shaping a more *inclusive collegium*, one based in trusting and respectful personal and professional relationships, expanded notions of expertise that recognize the contributions NTTF make to a shared mission on a daily basis, and a realistic assessment and understanding of the contexts in which faculty operate from the institutional to departmental levels.

Realizing this more inclusive collegium is, we believe, essential to a healthy higher education. The collegial ideal is difficult to attain, and perhaps even more so as the faculty changes and diversifies in not only role but also gender, race, ethnicity, sexual orientation, religion, and educational background. But this same ongoing evolution of the faculty makes the attention to collegiality all the more imperative, for it is the relationships, trust and respect, and professional regard that will allow higher education to navigate these changes and realize the many benefits of diversity. The challenge and question, then, is whether other departments, their institutions, and the faculty profession can recognize the importance of doing this work and muster the will to do it. We hope so.

# References

Alleman, N. F., & Haviland, D. (2014, November). *"I expect to be engaged as an equal": Collegiality expectations of full-time, non-tenure-track faculty members.* Paper presented at the meeting of the Association for the Study of Higher Education, Washington, DC.

Alleman, N. F., & Haviland, D. (2016). "I expect to be engaged as an equal": Collegiality expectations of full-time, non-tenure-track faculty members. *Higher Education 74*(3), 527–542. doi:10.1007/s10734-016-0062-4

Alleman, N. F., Holly, L. N., & Costello, C. A. (2013). Agency and influence: The organizational impact of a new school of education building. *Planning for Higher Education, 41*(2), 83–93. Retrieved from https://www.scup.org/resource/agency-and-influence/

American Association of University Professors. (2014). *Contingent appointments and the academic profession* [Press release]. Retrieved from https://www.aaup.org/report/contingent-appointments-and-academic-profession

American Association of University Professors. (2018). *Data snapshot: Contingent faculty in US higher ed.* Retrieved from https://www.aaup.org/news/data-snapshot-contingent-faculty-us-higher-ed#.XToYIfJKi70

Baldwin, R. G., & Chronister, J. L. (2001). *Teaching without tenure.* Baltimore, MD: Johns Hopkins University Press.

Barnes, L. L. B., Agago, M. O., & Coombs, W. T. (1998). Effects of job-related stress on faculty intention to leave academia. *Research in Higher Education, 39*(1), 457–469. doi: 10.1023/A:1018741404199

Becher, T. (1989). *Academic tribes and territories: Intellectual enquiry and the cultures of disciplines.* Bristol, PA: SRHE & Open University Press.

Bennett, J. B. (1998). *Collegial professionalism: The academy, individualism, and the common good* (American Council on Education & Oryx Press Series on Higher Education). Phoenix, AZ: Oryx Press.

Bergquist, W. H., & Pawlak, K. (2008). *Engaging the six cultures of the academy* (2nd ed.). San Francisco, CA: Jossey-Bass.

Bess, J. L. (1992). Collegiality: Toward a clarification of meaning and function. In J. C. Smart (Ed.), *Higher education: Handbook of theory and research* (Vol. 8, pp. 1–36). Dordrecht, Netherlands: Springer.

Birnbaum, R. (1988). *How colleges work: The cybernetics of academic organization and leadership*. San Francisco, CA: Jossey-Bass.

Bode, R. K. (1999). Mentoring and collegiality. In R. J. Menges (Ed.), *Faculty in new jobs: A guide to settling in, becoming established, and building institutional rapport* (pp. 118–144). San Francisco, CA: Jossey-Bass.

Boice, R. (1992). *The new faculty member: Supporting and fostering professional development*. San Francisco, CA: Jossey-Bass.

Bowen, H. R., & Schuster, J. H. (1986). *American professors: A national resource imperiled*. New York, NY: Oxford University Press.

Boyer, E. L. (1990). *College: The undergraduate experience in America*. New York, NY: Harper & Row.

Cipriano, R. E. (2011). *Facilitating a collegial department in higher education: Strategies for success*. San Francisco, CA: Jossey-Bass.

Clark, B. R. (1987). *The academic life: Small worlds, different worlds*. Princeton, NJ: The Carnegie Foundation for the Advancement of Teaching.

Cross, J. G., & Goldenberg, E. N. (2009). *Off-track profs: Nontenured teachers in higher education*. Cambridge, MA: The MIT Press.

Downey, J. (1996). The university as trinity: Balancing corporation, collegium, and community. *Innovative Higher Education, 21*(2), 73–85. doi:10.1007/BF01243699

Ehrenberg, R. G., & Zhang, L. (2005). Do tenured and tenure-track faculty matter? *The Journal of Human Resources, 40*(3), 647–659. Retrieved from https://www.jstor.org/stable/4129555

Finkelstein, M. J., Conley, V. M., & Schuster, J. H. (2016). *The faculty factor: Reassessing the American academy in a turbulent era*. Baltimore, MD: Johns Hopkins University Press.

Finkelstein, M. J., & Schuster, J. H. (2011). A new higher education: The "next model" takes shape. TIAA-CREF Institute. Retrieved from https://www.tiaainstitute.org/sites/default/files/presentations/2017-02/ahe_nextmodel0411.pdf

Gappa, J. M., Austin, A. E., & Trice, A. G. (2005). Rethinking academic work and workplaces. *Change, 37*(6), 32–39. doi:10/3200/CHNG.37.6.32-29

Gappa, J. M., Austin, A. E., & Trice, A. G. (2007). *Rethinking faculty work: Higher education's strategic imperative*. San Francisco, CA: Jossey-Bass.

Gieryn, T. F. (2002). What buildings do. *Theory and Society, 31*(1), 35–74. doi:10.1023/A:1014404201290

Golde, C. M., & Dore, T. M. (2001). *At cross purposes: What the experiences of today's doctoral students reveal about doctoral education*. Philiadelphia, PA: The Pew Charitable Trust. Retrieved from https://files.eric.ed.gov/fulltext/ED450628.pdf

Hardy, C. (1991). Pluralism, power and collegiality in universities. *Financial Accountability and Management, 7*(3), 127–142. doi: 10.1111/j.1468-0408.1991.tb00346.x

Haviland, D., Alleman, N., & Cliburn Allen, C. (2017). "Separate but not quite equal": Collegiality experiences of full-time, non-tenure-track faculty members. *The Journal of Higher Education, 88*(4), 505–528. doi:10.1080/00221546.2016 .1272321

Hearn, J. C., & Deupree, M. M. (2013). Here today, gone tomorrow: The increasingly contingent faculty workforce. *TIAA-CREF Institute: Advancing Higher Education.* Retrieved from https://www.tiaa-crefinstitute.org/public/institute/ research/advancing_higher_education/contingentfaculty0313.html

Hollenshead, C., Waltman, J., August, L., Miller, J., Smith, G., & Bell, A. (2007). *Making the best of both worlds: Findings from a national institution-level survey of non-tenure track faculty.* Ann Arbor, MI: Center for the Education of Women. Retrieved from http://www.cew.umich.edu/library/cew-research-publications/

Jaeger, A. J., & Eagan, M. K. (2011). Examining retention and contingent faculty use in a state system of public higher education. *Educational Policy, 25*(3), 507– 537. doi:10.1177/0895904810361723

Kezar, A. (2012). *Embracing non-tenure track faculty: Changing campuses for the new faculty majority.* New York, NY: Routledge.

Kezar, A. (2013a). *Changing faculty workforce models.* Retrieved from https://www .tiaa.org/public/pdf/changing-faculty-workforce-models.pdf

Kezar, A. (2013b). Department cultures and non-tenure-track faculty: Willingness, capacity, and opportunity to perform at four-year institutions. *Journal of Higher Education, 84*(3), 153–188. doi: 10.1353/jhe.2013.0011

Kezar, A. (2013c). Examining non-tenure track faculty perceptions of how departmental policies and practices shape their performance and ability to create student learning at four-year institutions. *Research in Higher Education, 54*(5), 571–598. doi:10.1007/s11162-013-9288-5

Kezar, A. (2013d). Non-tenure-track faculty's social construction of a supportive work environment. *Teachers College Record, 115*(12), 47. Retrieved from https:// www.tcrecord.org/library/content.asp?contentid=17242

Kezar, A., & Maxey, D. (2013). The changing academic workforce. *Trusteeship, 21*(3), 1–12. Retrieved from https://agb.org/trusteeship-article/the-changing-academic-workforce/

Kezar, A., & Maxey, D. (2015). *Adapting by design: Creating faculty roles and defining faculty work to ensure an intentional future for colleges and universities.* Los Angeles, CA: The Delphi Project on the Changing Faculty and Student Success. Retrieved from http://www.uscrossier.org/pullias/wp-content/uploads/2015/06/DELPHI-PROJECT_ADAPTING-BY-DESIGN_2ED.pdf

Kezar, A., Maxey, D., & Eaton, J. S. (2014). *An examination of the changing faculty: Ensuring institutional quality and achieving desired student learning outcomes.* Paper presented at the Institute for Research and Study of Accreditation and Quality Assurance, Washington DC. Retrieved from http://www.uscrossier.org/pullias/wp-content/uploads/2014/01/CHEA_Examination_Changing_Faculty_2013.pdf

Kezar, A., & Sam, C. (2010a). Non-tenure track faculty in higher education: Theories and tensions. *ASHE Higher Education Report* (Vol. 36, No. 3). San Francisco, CA: Jossey-Bass. doi: 10.1002/aehe.3605

Kezar, A., & Sam, C. (2010b). Understanding the new majority of non-tenure-track faculty in higher education: Demographics, experiences, and plans of action. *ASHE Higher Education Report* (Vol. 36, No. 4). San Francisco, CA: Jossey-Bass. doi: 10.1002/aehe.3604

Kezar, A., & Sam, C. (2011). Understanding non-tenure track faculty: New assumptions and theories for conceptualizing behavior. *American Behavioral Scientist, 55*(11), 1419–1442. doi:10.1177/0002764211408879

Levin, J. S., & Shaker, G. G. (2011). The hybrid and dualistic identity of full-time non-tenure-track faculty. *American Behavioral Scientist, 55*(11), 1461–1484. doi:10.1177/0002764211409382

Mangiardi, J., & Pellegrino, E. (1992). Collegiality: What is it? *Bulletin of the New York Academy of Medicine, 68*(2), 292–296.

Maxey, D., & Kezar, A. (2015). Revealing opportunities and obstacles for changing non-tenure-track faculty practices: An examination of stakeholders' awareness of institutional contradictions. *Journal of Higher Education, 86*(4), 564–594. doi: 10.1080/00221546.2015.11777375

Ott, M., & Cisneros, J. (2015). Understanding the changing faculty workforce in higher education: A comparison of full-time non-tenure track and tenure line experiences. *Education Policy Analysis Archives, 23*(90), 1–28. http://dx.doi.org/10.14507/epaa.v23.1934

Petro, J. A. (1992). Collegiality in history. *Bulletin of the New York Academy of Medicine, 68*(2), 286–291. Retrieved from https://www.ncbi.nlm.nih.gov/pmc/articles/PMC1810169/

Prieber, C. L. (1991). *The authority of collegiality: The history of university faculty and the dialectic in the recognition of higher knowledge* (Doctoral dissertation). Retrieved from ProQuest (Order No. 9135127).

Rice, R. E. (1986). The academic profession in transition: Toward a new social fiction. *Teaching Sociology, 14*(1), 12–23. doi:10.2307/1318295

Rice, R. E., Sorcinelli, M. D., & Austin, A. E. (2000). Heeding new voices: Academic careers for a new generation. *New Pathways Working Paper Series* (Vol. 7). Washington, DC: American Association of Higher Education.

Schuster, J. H., & Finkelstein, M. J. (2006). *The American faculty: The restructuring of academic work and careers.* Baltimore, MD: Johns Hopkins Univeristy Press.

Stewart, A., & Valian, V. (2018). *An inclusive academy: Achieving diversity and excellence.* Cambridge, MA: MIT Press.

Tierney, W. G. (2008). Trust and organizational culture in higher education. In J. Välimaa & O. H. Ylijoki (Eds.), *Cultural perspectives on higher education* (pp. 27–41). Dordrecht, NL: Springer.

Tierney, W. G., & Bensimon, E. M. (1996). *Promotion and tenure: Community and socialization in academe.* Albany, NY: State University of New York Press.

Turner, C. S. V., & Myers Jr., S. L. (2000). *Faculty of color in academe: Bittersweet success.* Boston, MA: Allyn & Bacon.

Umber, A. (2014, August 20). I used to be a good teacher. *The Chronicle of Higher Education.* Retrieved from https://chroniclevitae.com/news/668-i-used-to-be-a-good-teacher

U.S. Department of Education, National Center for Education Statistics (NCES). (2018). *IPEDS: Integrated Postsecondary Education Data System: Spring 2016 through Spring 2018 Human Resources component*, Fall Staff section. (Table prepared November 2018.) Retrieved from https://nces.ed.gov/programs/digest/d18/tables/dt18_315.20.asp

U.S. Government Accountability Office (GAO). (2017). *Contingent workforce: Size, characteristics, compensation, and work experiences of adjunct and other non-tenure-track faculty* (Report No. 18-49). Retrieved from https://www.gao.gov/assets/690/687871.pdf

Wagoner, J. L., & Kellams, S. E. (1992). Professoriate: History and status. In B. R. Clark & G. Neave (Eds.), *The encyclopedia of higher education* (Vol. 3, pp. 1674–1686). Oxford, England: Pergamon Press.

Waltman, J., Bergom, I., Hollenshead, C., Miller, J., & August, L. (2012). Factors contributing to job satisfaction and dissatisfaction among non-tenure-track faculty. *The Journal of Higher Education, 83*(3), 411–434. doi: 10.1353/jhe.2012.0014

# About the Authors

**Don Haviland** is professor and chair of the educational leadership department at California State University, Long Beach. His recent research focuses on faculty development. He has coauthored (with Nathan Alleman and Cara Cliburn Allen) a recent ASHE monograph titled *Collegiality and the Collegium in an Era of Faculty Differentiation* (Wiley, 2017), a book for early career faculty titled *Shaping Your Career: A Guide for Early Career Faculty* (Stylus Publishing, 2017) with Anna Ortiz and Laura Henriques, and multiple articles related to faculty.

**Jenny Jacobs,** (she/her/hers/herself), EdD, is an adjunct professor of theater who has served undergraduate and graduate programs at institutions on the east and west coasts including Temple University, Rider University, Cypress College, and Chapman University. Jacobs's own research focuses on the value of the performing arts in higher education, and she most recently contributed to *Student Affairs in Urban Serving Institutions* (Routledge, 2019) as chapter author and assisted Don Haviland and his coauthors with the production of *Shaping Your Career: A Guide for Early Career Faculty* (Stylus Publishing, 2017).

**Nathan F. Alleman**, PhD, is associate professor in the higher education studies program at Baylor University and a research fellow with the Texas Hunger Initiative. His work focuses on marginal and marginalized populations and institutions and has appeared in journals such as *Research in Higher Education*, the *Journal of College Student Development*, and the *Journal of Higher Education*. Recent faculty scholarship includes an ASHE monograph titled *Collegiality and the Collegium in an Era of Faculty Differentiation* (Wiley, 2017) with Cara Cliburn Allen and Don Haviland. Other recent books include *The Outrageous Idea of Christian Teaching* (Oxford University Press, 2019) with Perry Glanzer.

**Cara Cliburn Allen** is a doctoral candidate in the higher education studies and leadership program at Baylor University. Cliburn Allen studies the success factors of various subpopulations in higher education, including faculty (nontenure-track faculty and faculty denied tenure), underrepresented students (food insecure, community college), and student affairs administrators. With coauthors Nathan F. Alleman and Don Haviland, she has published an ASHE monograph, *Collegiality and the Collegium in an Era of Faculty Differentiation* (Wiley, 2017), and multiple articles detailing the experiences and expectations of full-time nontenure-track faculty.

minoritized faculty, 5, 12, 24–27, 30
MU. *See* Master's University

National Center for Education
    Statistics, 5
NTTF. *See* full-time non-tenure-track
    faculty

professional expertise, recognition of,
    16, 56, 70, 86
  academic governance participation
    and, 46, 48
  administrative or teaching work
    affirmation in, 49
  administrative positions and
    leadership opportunities in, 42–43
  collegiality concept in, 8, 10
  cultural shifts needed in, 53
  cultural workarounds in, 48
  curriculum shaping in, 46–47
  departmental aims contribution in,
    38
  department chair key figure in, 37,
    45, 47–48
  department chairs recommendations
    for, 54–55
  department meeting participation
    in, 47
  educational preparation value in, 39
  evaluation job description and form
    use in, 50–51
  expanded conceptions of, 37
  faculty training and curriculum
    decision-making in, 39
  formal award creation for, 49–50, 82
  hierarchy reduction in, 38
  hiring decision participation policies
    in, 48
  industry experience contribution in,
    37
  industry expertise conversations in,
    40–41
  institutional guidance in, 53
  institutional policies and, 36, 37, 47

  intentionality in, 82
  long industry careers and, 40
  master's and doctorate degrees and,
    40
  merit pay metrics and, 51
  NTTF and TTF course teaching in,
    38
  NTTF as instructional role experts
    in, 37
  NTTF committee service areas and
    value of, 46–47
  NTTF evaluation weakness in, 50
  NTTF lack of opportunity in, 81
  NTTF pathway absence in, 11
  NTTF sabbatical applications and,
    44
  NTTF task force creation and policy
    change in, 52
  NTTF upper-level course teaching
    and, 38–39
  pay alignment with, 51
  pay equity lack in, 51
  peer evaluation and advancement
    opportunities in, 50
  personal interests and expertise
    alignment in, 42
  policy and practice difference
    diminishing in, 52
  professional development funding
    and NTTF support in, 43–44
  professional growth cautions in, 45
  professional growth opportunities
    and, 41
  promotion review committees in, 50
  public affirmation of, 49
  research and course releases in,
    41–42
  research pressure and pay increase
    in, 42
  same title reference in, 52
  scholarship driven in, 36
  service caution in, 47
  shared governance participation in,
    36

teaching and professional experience in, 36

teaching development grant-funded initiative example in, 43

teaching equal to research in, 36

tenure-normative model work around in, 81

tenure-track faculty recommendations for, 55

terminal degree relationship change example in, 39–40

TTF and NTTF faculty development opportunities in, 44–45

TTF process for earning, 81

TTF support and consulting of NTTF in, 52

universities and departments nurturing of, 82

university administrators recommendations for, 54

recommendations
for institutional context leveraging, 75–76
for interpersonal trust and respect cultivation, 33–35
for professional expertise recognition, 54–55

research, 2, 36, 41–42, 58, 65–66

research study
collegial space shaping in, 14
data on, 14
disciplines in, 14
driving purpose of, 15
first and second phases of, 14
gender in, 14
NTTF insights in, 14–15
participant characteristics in, 14
positive collegial spaces in, 17
primary audience for, 15
racial and ethnic diversity in, 14
"what works" focus in, 15

Research University (RU), 1, 14, 57–59

Rice, R. E., 86

RU. *See* Research University

shared mission, 7–8, 27, 29, 33, 36, 83, 91

social identities and relationships, 15, 31–32
diversity and collegiality tension in, 27
faculty recognition of inequities in, 25
interpersonal interactions complications in, 24
issues of, 24
minoritized faculty careful and cautious in, 26–27
minoritized population identity significance in, 24–25
substantial service inequity in, 25
traditional homogeneity challenging in, 26
women of color experiences in, 26–27
work and contributions not valued in, 25

Social Science Department (MU)
collegiality wane in, 62
department chair culture change at, 61
freeway flyers hiring in, 61
institutional competing expectations in, 61
lecturers instructional role in, 61
mailbox assignments symbolic message in, 60
name cards in, 60
NTTF contribution expectation at, 61–62
office distribution and space challenges of, 59
office sharing opportunities and liabilities in, 60
part-time faculty turnover in, 60
same building importance in, 59–60

*Faculty Development books from Stylus Publishing*

**Advancing the Culture of Teaching on Campus**
*ow a Teaching Center Can Make a Difference*
Edited by Constance Cook and Matthew Kaplan
Foreword by Lester P. Monts

**Faculty Mentoring**
*A Practical Manual for Mentors, Mentees, Administrators, and Faculty Developers*
Susan L. Phillips and Susan T. Dennison
Foreword by Milton D. Cox

**Faculty Retirement**
*Best Practices for Navigating the Transition*
Edited by Claire Van Ummersen, Jean McLaughlin and Lauren Duranleau
Foreword by Lotte Bailyn

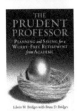

**The Prudent Professor**
*Planning and Saving for a Worry-Free Retirement from Academe*
Edwin M. Bridges and Brian D. Bridges

**Teaching Across Cultural Strengths**
*A Guide to Balancing Integrated and Individuated Cultural Frameworks in College Teaching*
Alicia Fedelina Chávez and Susan Diana Longerbeam
Foreword by Joseph L. White

**Why Students Resist Learning**
*A Practical Model for Understanding and Helping Students*
Edited by Anton O. Tolman and Janine Kremling
Foreword by John Tagg

*Graduate and Doctoral Education books from Stylus Publishing*

**From Diplomas to Doctorates**
*The Success of Black Women in Higher Education and its Implications for Equal Educational Opportunities for All*
Edited by V. Barbara Bush, Crystal Renee Chambers, and Mary Beth Walpole

**The Latina/o Pathway to the Ph.D.**
*Abriendo Caminos*
Edited by Jeanett Castellanos, Alberta M. Gloria, and Mark Kamimura
Foreword by Melba Vasquez and Hector Garza

**On Becoming a Scholar**
*Socialization and Development in Doctoral Education*
Jay Caulfield
Edited by Susan K. Gardner and Pilar Mendoza
Foreword by Ann E. Austin and Kevin Kruger

**Developing Quality Dissertations in the Humanities**
*A Graduate Student's Guide to Achieving Excellence*
Barbara E. Lovitts and Ellen L. Wert

**Developing Quality Dissertations in the Sciences**
*A Graduate Student's Guide to Achieving Excellence*
Barbara E. Lovitts and Ellen L. Wert

**Developing Quality Dissertations in the Social Sciences**
*A Graduate Student's Guide to Achieving Excellence*
Barbara E. Lovitts and Ellen L. Wert

*Professional Development books from Stylus Publishing*

**Adjunct Faculty Voices**
*Cultivating Professional Development and Community at the Front Lines of Higher Education*
Edited by Roy Fuller, Marie Kendall Brown and Kimberly Smith
Foreword by Adrianna Kezar

**Authoring Your Life**
*Developing an INTERNAL VOICE to Navigate Life's Challenges*
Marcia B. Baxter Magolda
Foreword by Sharon Daloz Parks
Illustrated by Matthew Henry Hall

**The Coach's Guide for Women Professors**
*Who Want a Successful Career and a Well-Balanced Life*
Rena Seltzer
Foreword by Frances Rosenbluth

**Contingent Academic Labor**
*Evaluating Conditions to Improve Student Outcomes*
Daniel B. Davis
Foreword by Adrianna Kezar

**Shaping Your Career**
*A Guide for Early Career Faculty*
Don Haviland, Anna M. Ortiz and Laura Henriques
Foreword by Ann E. Austin

**What They Didn't Teach You in Graduate School**
*299 Helpful Hints for Success in Your Academic Career*
Paul Gray and David E. Drew Illustrated by Matthew Henry Hall
Foreword by Laurie Richlin and Steadman Upham

*Race & Diversity books from Stylus Publishing*

**Advancing Black Male Student Success From Preschool Through Ph.D.**
Edited by Shaun R. Harper and J. Luke Wood

**Everyday White People Confront Racial and Social Injustice**
*15 Stories*
Edited by Eddie Moore, Jr., Marguerite W. Penick-Parks and Ali Michael
Foreword by Paul C. Gorski

**The Diversity Consultant Cookbook**
*Preparing for the Challenge*
Written and Edited by Eddie Moore, Jr., Art Munin, and Marguerite W. Penick-Parks
Foreword by Jamie Washington
Afterword by Joey Iazzetto

**Critical Race Spatial Analysis**
*Mapping to Understand and Address Educational Inequity*
Edited by Deb Morrison, Subini Ancy Annamma, and Darrell D. Jackson

**Closing the Opportunity Gap**
*Identity-Conscious Strategies for Retention and Student Success*
Edited by Vijay Pendakur
Foreword by Shaun R. Harper

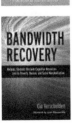

**Bandwidth Recovery**
*Helping Students Reclaim Cognitive Resources Lost to Poverty, Racism, and Social Marginalization*
Cia Verschelden
Foreword by Lynn Pasquerella

prescriptions for change will not be ignored by the vast majority of the intended audience: administrators and trustees. The rest of us with a stake in higher education cannot afford to ignore this book and its very reasonable ideas for change. I look forward to his next book about how to get there." — **Joe T. Berry**, *author*, Reclaiming the Ivory Tower; *editor of the weekly news aggregator* COCAL Updates

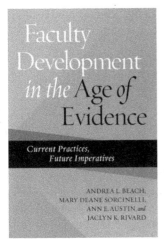

### Faculty Development in the Age of Evidence

*Current Practices, Future Imperatives*

Andrea L. Beach, Mary Deane Sorcinelli, Ann E. Austin, and Jaclyn K. Rivard

"Overall, *Faculty Development in the Age of Evidence* is an essential resource for the field of faculty development and for the higher education sector. Beach and colleagues provide an updated examination of the status of the field and create meaningful arguments in favor of continually strengthening faculty development. Beyond that, the book asks important questions for practitioners to reflect and act upon in order to continue evolving the field of faculty development and the overall impact of higher education in society." — ***Teachers College Record***

22883 Quicksilver Drive
Sterling, VA 20166-2019

Subscribe to our e-mail alerts: www.Styluspub.com

*Also available from Stylus*

## Adjunct Faculty Voices

*Cultivating Professional Development and Community at the Front Lines of Higher Education*

Edited by Roy Fuller, Marie Kendall Brown, and Kimberly Smith

Foreword by Adrianna Kezar

"This book is a lucid analysis of the adjunct faculty crisis. It adds to the literature by updating the taxonomy of adjuncts in useful ways, but it is not just an academic exercise. Finally, a book that gives voice to contingent faculty themselves, their struggles and their accomplishments. The four areas for improvement identified—identification/recruitment, community, equity, and development—are followed up with replicable models. A remarkable work, appealing to both adjunct faculty and administrators!" — *Michele DiPietro*, *Executive Director, Faculty Development and Recognition, Center for Excellence in Teaching and Learning, Kennesaw State University*

## Contingent Academic Labor

*Evaluating Conditions to Improve Student Outcomes*

Daniel Davis

Foreword by Adrianna Kezar

"Daniel Davis got the single most important thing about current contingent faculty right (besides their extreme exploitation, of course), which is that most of us would rather be full-time, job-secure (tenured or otherwise) faculty. It is amazing how many writers get that wrong. One could hope that most of the book's cogent

*(continued on preceding page)*